AF349275

THE LIFE AND TIMES OF FOREVER

With love to the compassionate and tenacious team

that helped me to complete *The Life and Times of Forever*.

The book could not have existed or been finished without you.

That is my truth.

THE LIFE AND TIMES OF
FOREVER

a personal journal

PHOTOGRAPHS AND WORDS
PATRICIA Z. SMITH

OTHER TEXTS
KAREN C. FOX
KAREN ZACHARIAS

EDITOR
KAREN C. FOX

DESIGN
LOUISE BRODY

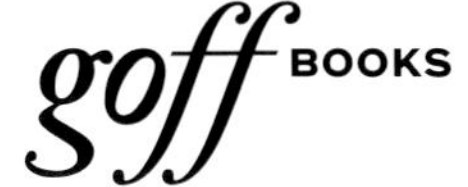

More important than how you go through life

is how life goes through you.

Message from the cosmos to PZS, dawn 2011

AUTHOR'S NOTE

A week after my 81st birthday I was diagnosed with COVID.
A year later—after countless tests and specialists—the
diagnosis became "an unidentifiable aggressive member
of the Parkinson PLUS family. There is no cure."

I have Parkinson's symptoms but NOT Parkinson's Disease
per se. It has the debilitating characteristics of Parkinson's.
My physical and cognitive abilities have declined quickly. I use
a battery–operated wheelchair. My lifeline has been shortened.

I returned to this book to finish it. Photos were taken on an
iPhone 13 Pro Max.

This book is a journal. It contains four sections: Phenomena,
Sea Turtle Art School, Gathering Flowers, and Food Worship.

PATRICIA Z. SMITH

"The past is the prologue."

William Shakespeare

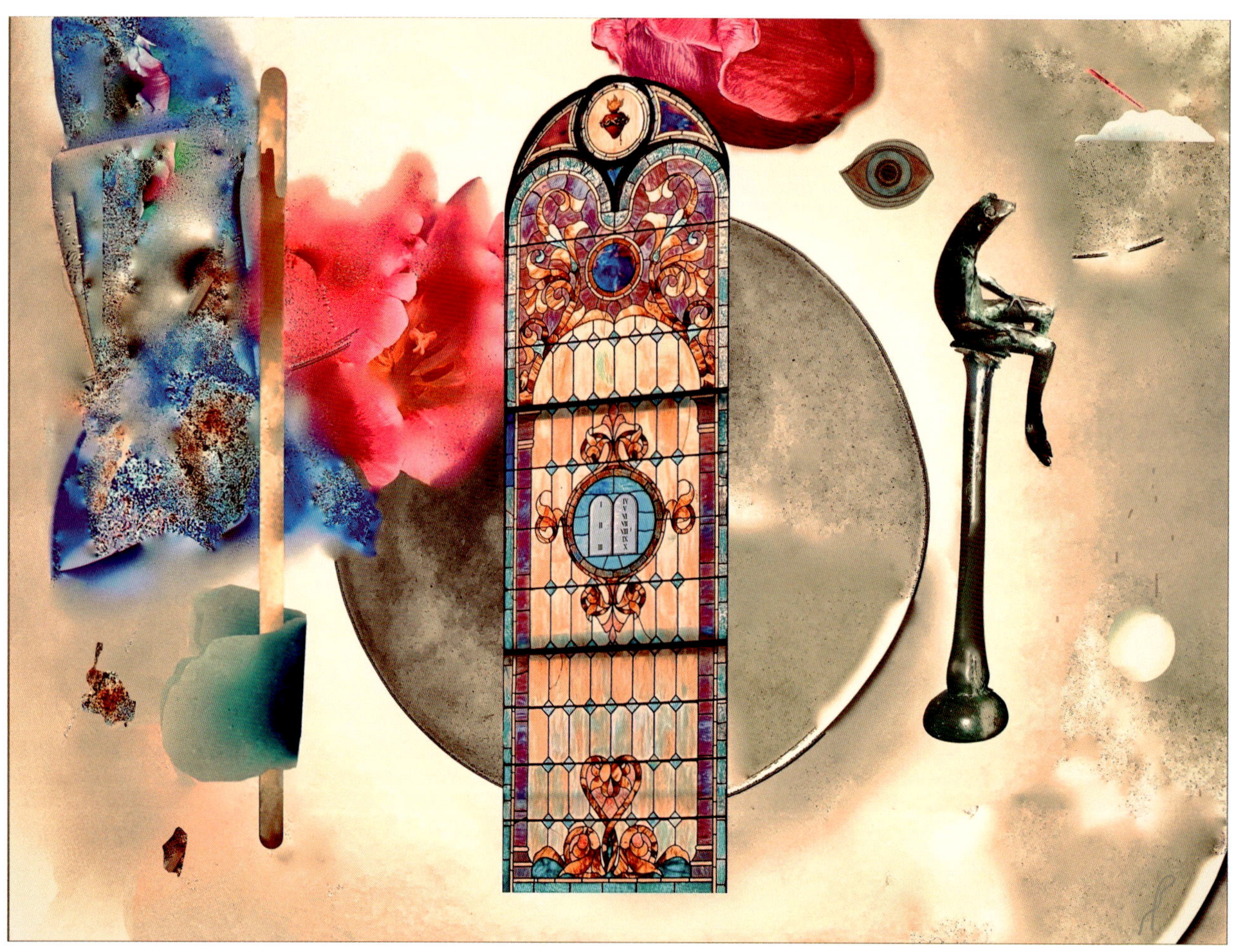

Remembering and wondering.

PHENOMENA

Time is an arrow. Or at least that's how physicists describe it. It goes in only one direction. We experience this in all sorts of ways—we can remember the past, but not see into the future, for one. But it's also tucked into the laws of entropy, that classic rule that everything in the world tends toward chaos. We see the cream we pour into our coffee swirl into the drink, but never see it reverse direction, coalescing into a single spot. We watch a glass break, but never see it slowly reassemble itself. Always, always we experience time moving in a single direction.

But, oh, how I've always wished we could see snatches of time stacked up on each other. I would have loved to walk by my old high school with my daughter, not only to remember who I had been when I was younger in that same place, but to have been able—when I was younger—to catch a quick vision of me now. To have had a flash-forward when I was at school of my same self, coming by later, a different person, having created an all-new family. I want to see layers of time as I stand in a single spot—just vague glimpses, I'm not greedy—looking forward, looking back, seeing repeated versions of myself, a different person at different moments.

Looking at those layers of moments, if only in my imagination, I know that I am not still who I was in the past. Yet, I can never be removed from how it shaped me. The arrow of time may only go in one direction, but it is all those moments—remembered willy nilly, collaged, and overlapping, not in some steadily marching-forward straight line—that create a whole person.

These collages—with photos captured, edited, created, massaged by my mother, who was called "Forever" when I was young—is a dance through life in a similar way. Each image is, of course, frozen in time, but comprises layers of color, forms, and information that make it appear to be in a state of transformation, which makes each image simultaneously evoke both static and overlapping moments of time.

The images manage to represent both the fleeting nature of the present while providing an elusive glimpse of past and future that adds up to form a whole: a whole person, a whole story, a whole artistic vision, helping us overcome the tyranny of time's arrow.

KAREN C. FOX
Science Writer. Author, *Older Than The Stars*

DAWN, ON THE WAY TO POMPEII, ITALY

Few places offer up a volcano like Vesuvius—
    death by fire, carapace of ash.

Humans preserved beside dogs and jugs of spice,
beneath murals so sensual they hit you behind the knees
and bring you to the ground,

so delicate you rise up again, and dance your spring dance
in Pompeii's pink, white, and yellow gardens.

                                  PZS

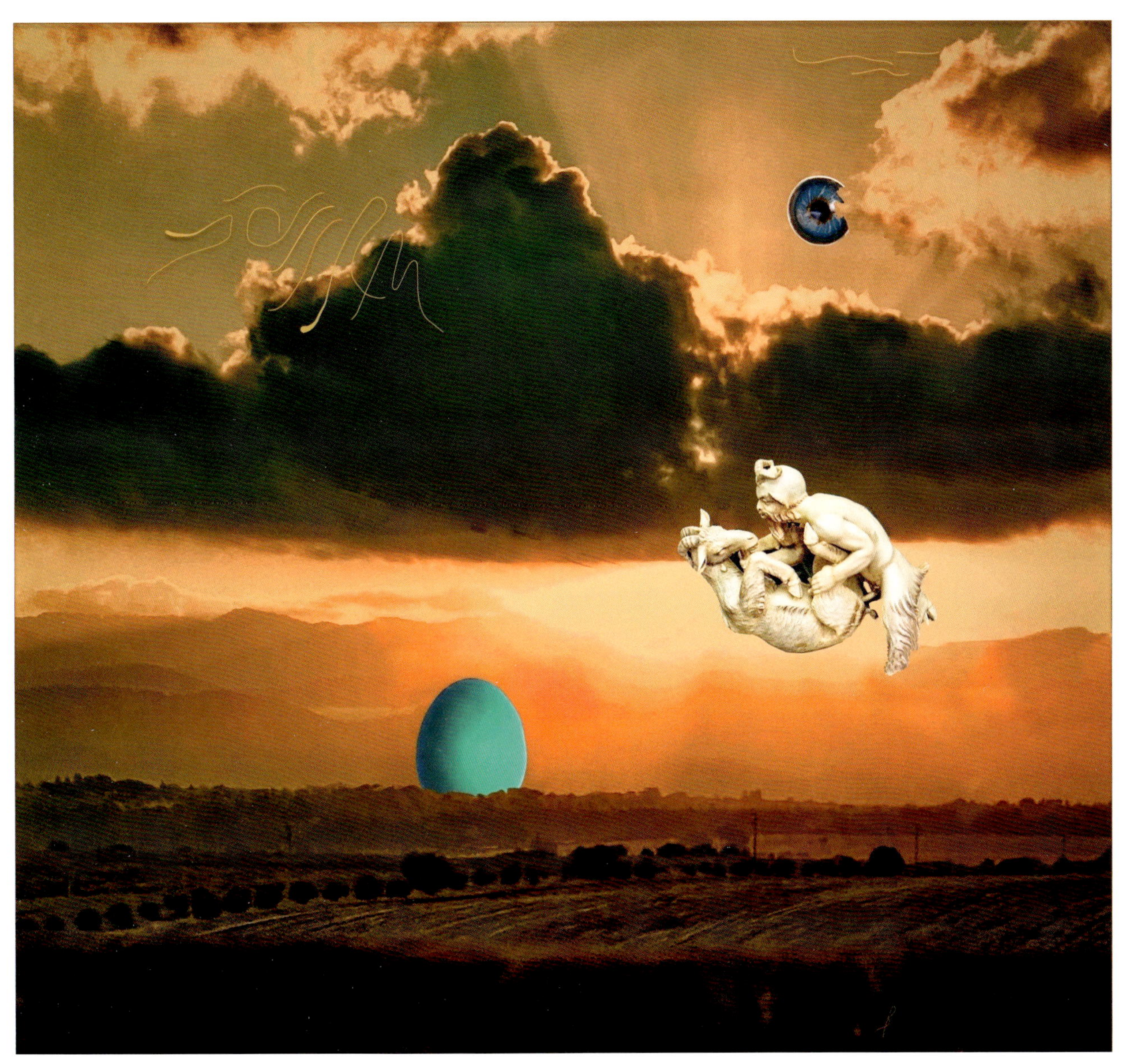

On the way to Pompeii, Italy.

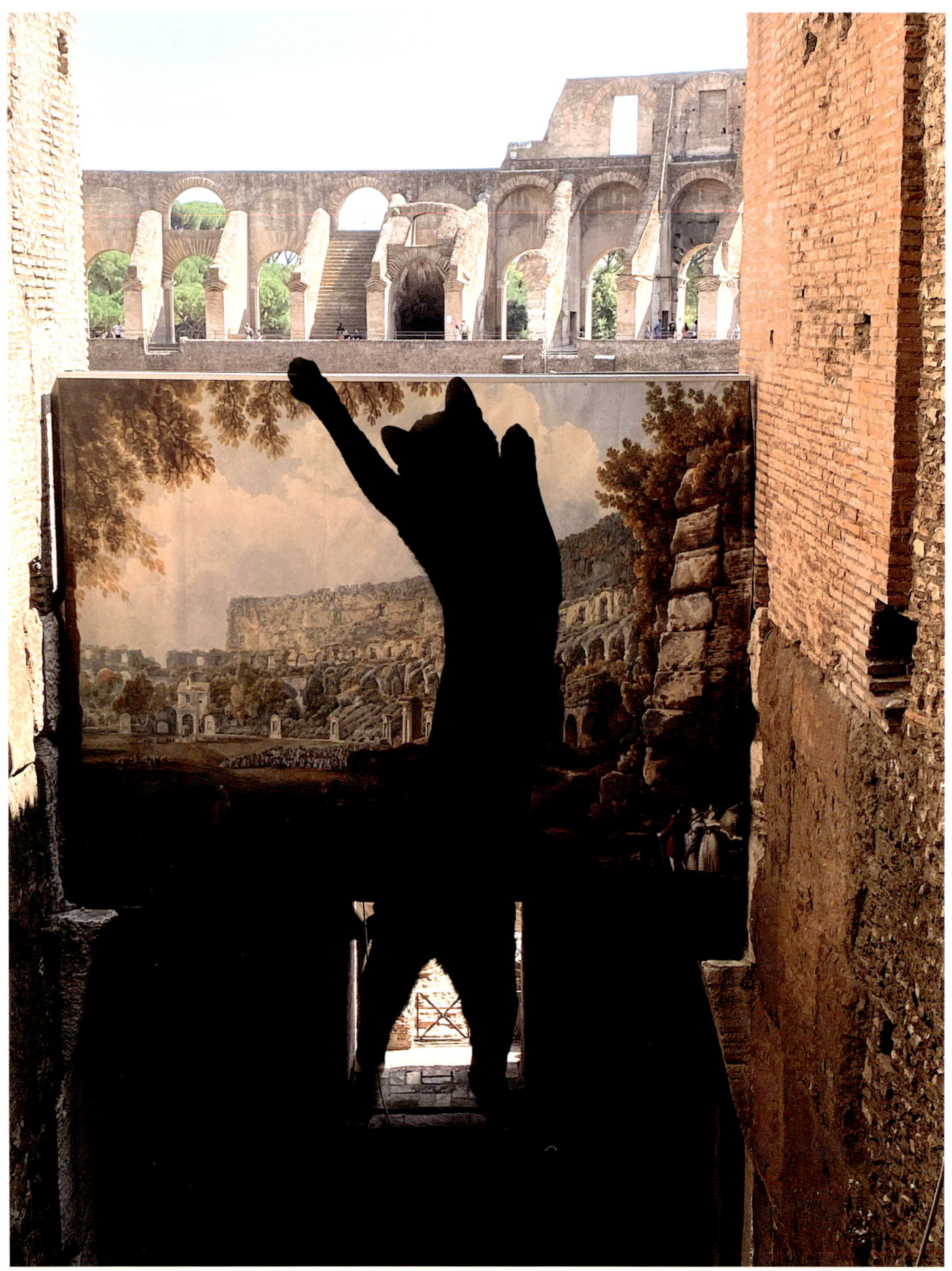

Curious cat at Coliseum, Rome.

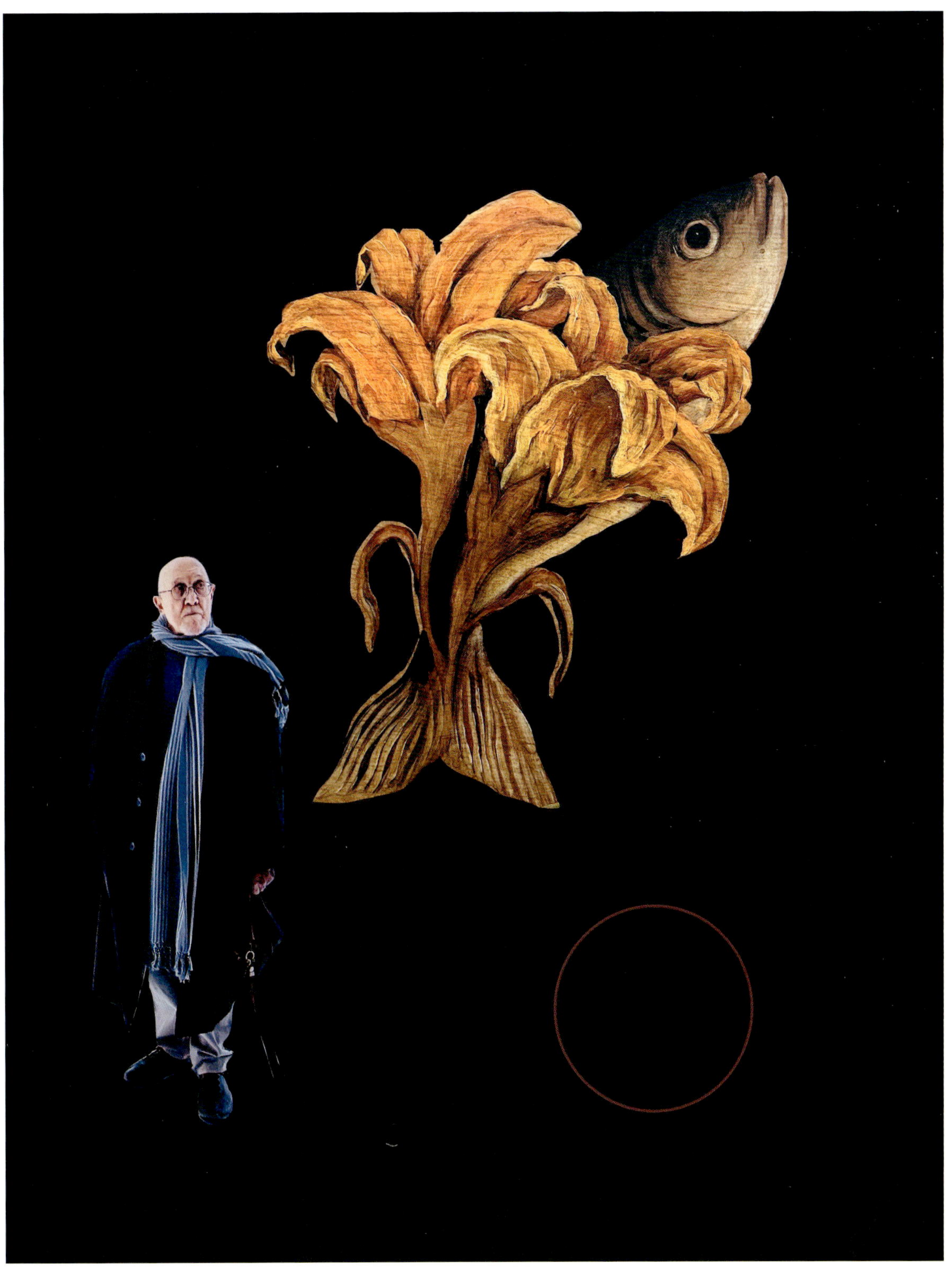

The one that got away.

Beauty is sometimes scary.

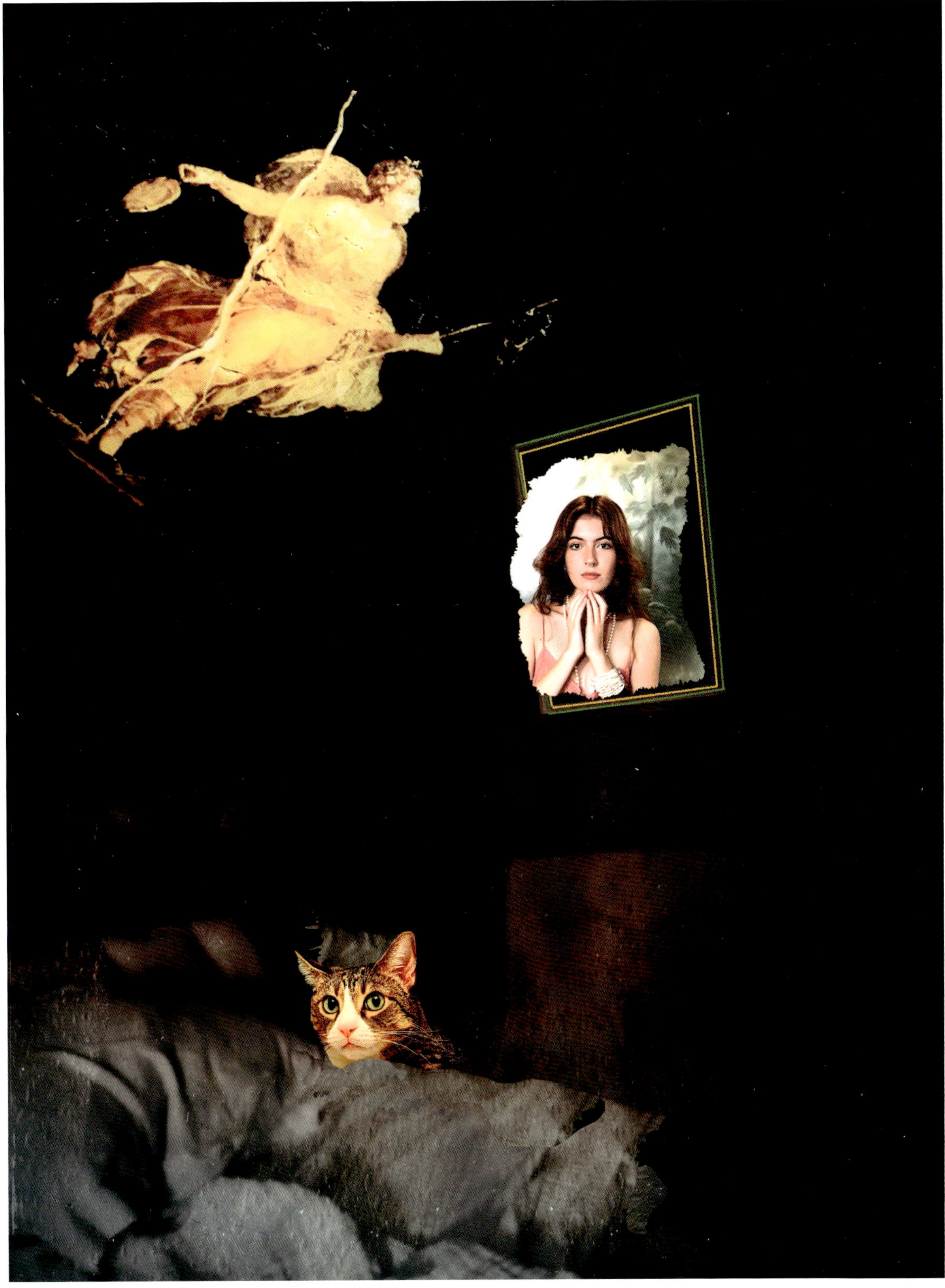

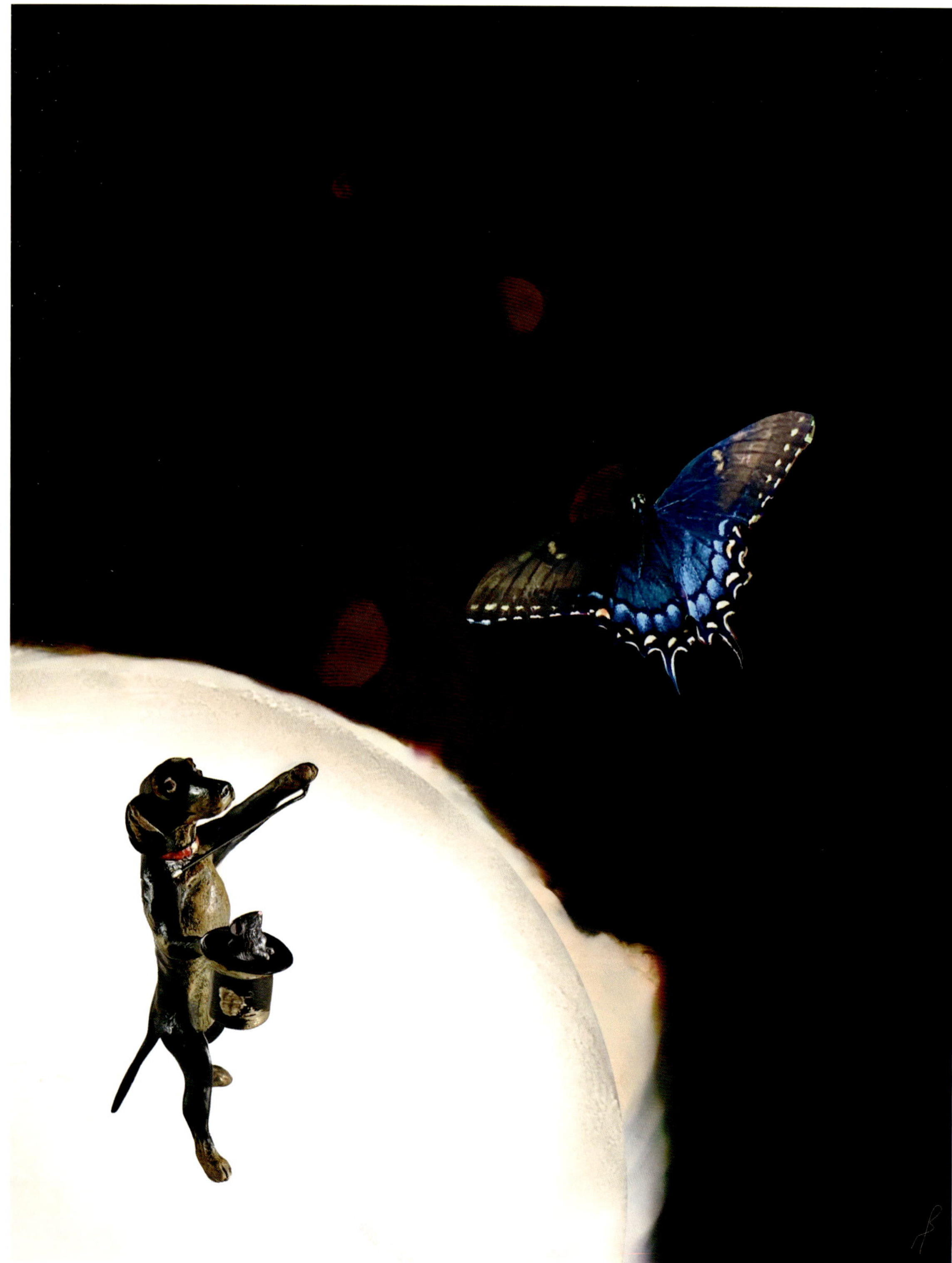

The butterfly diva.

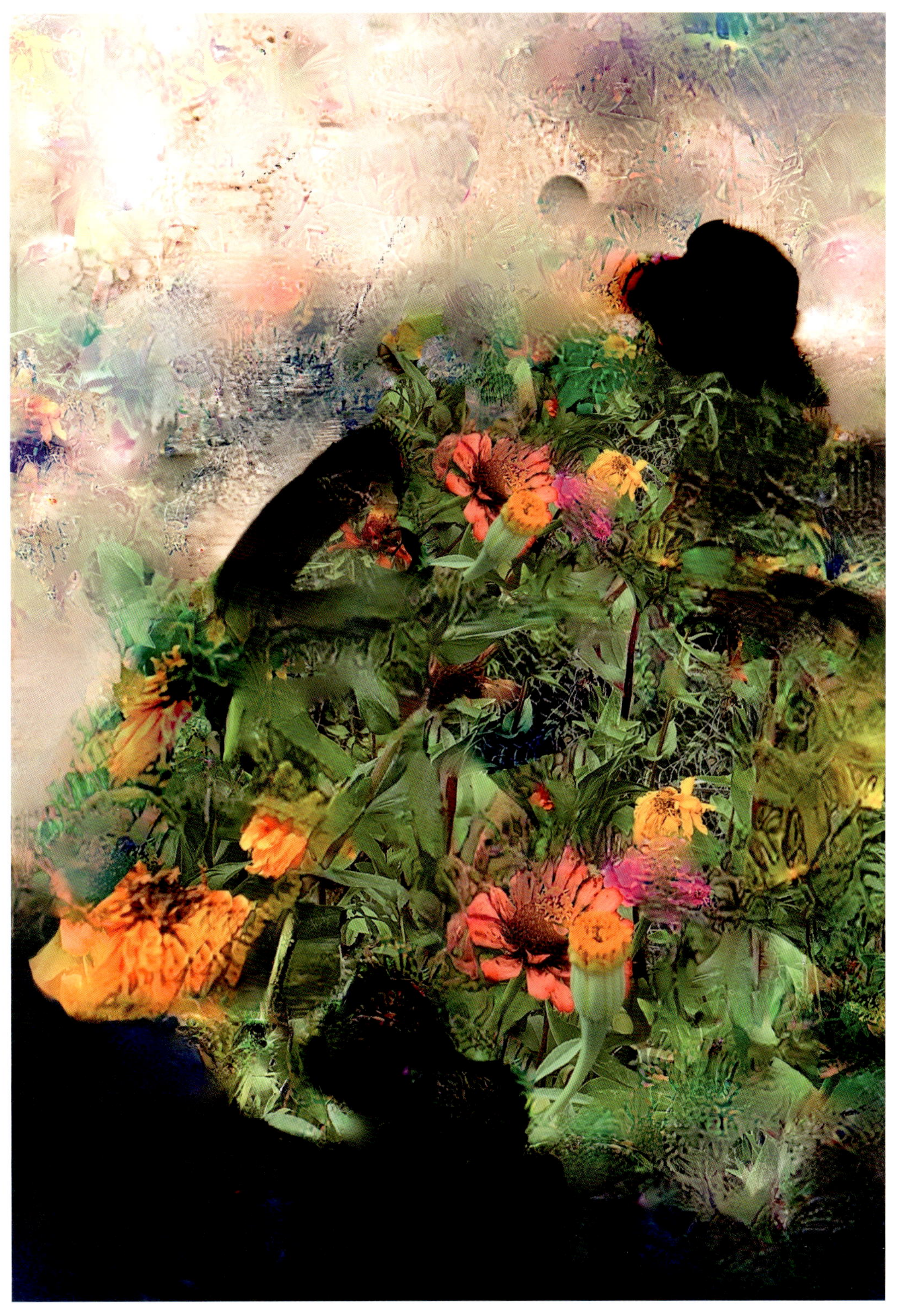

A moon tumble of flowers.

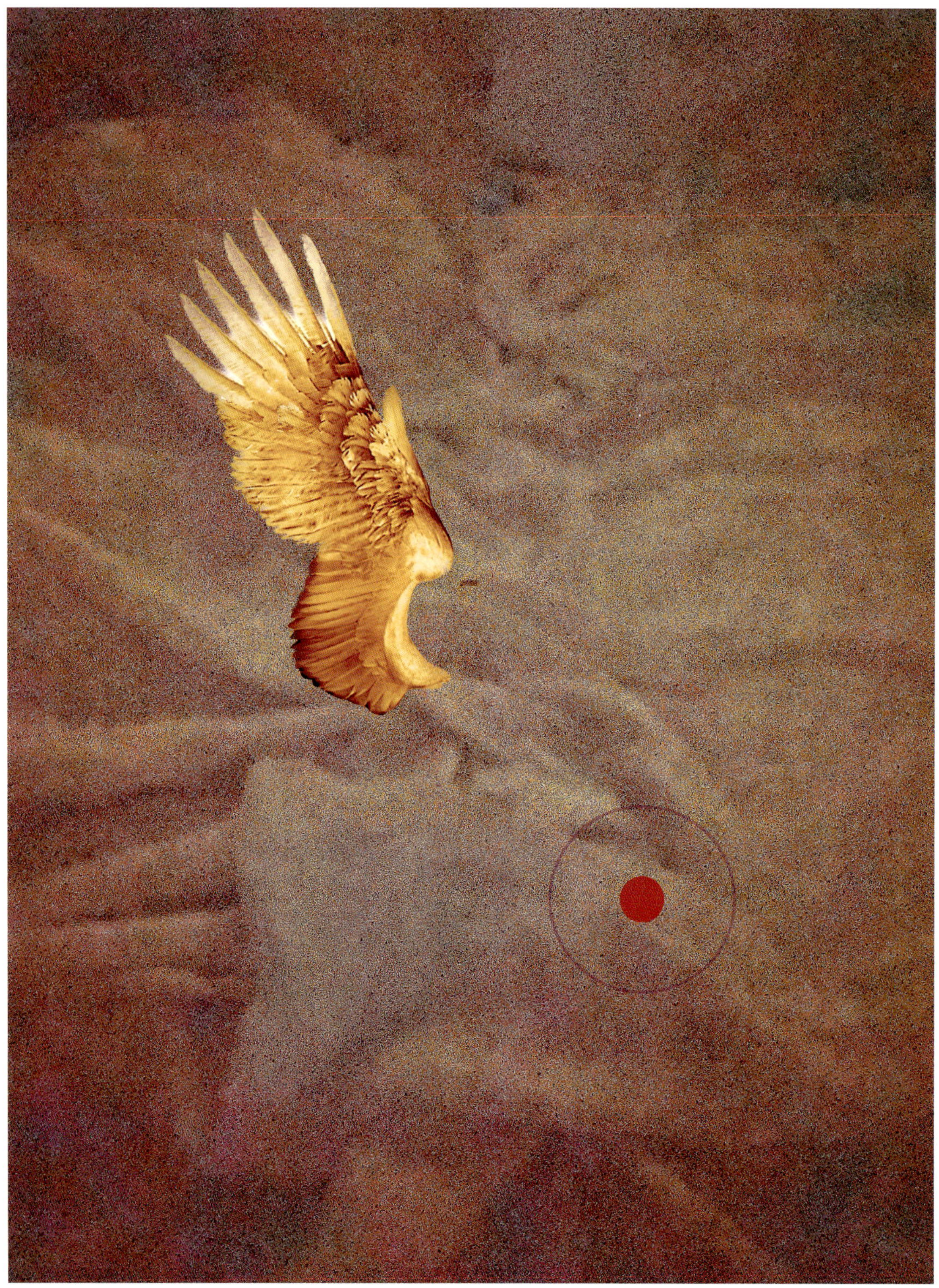

Flyaway wings . . .

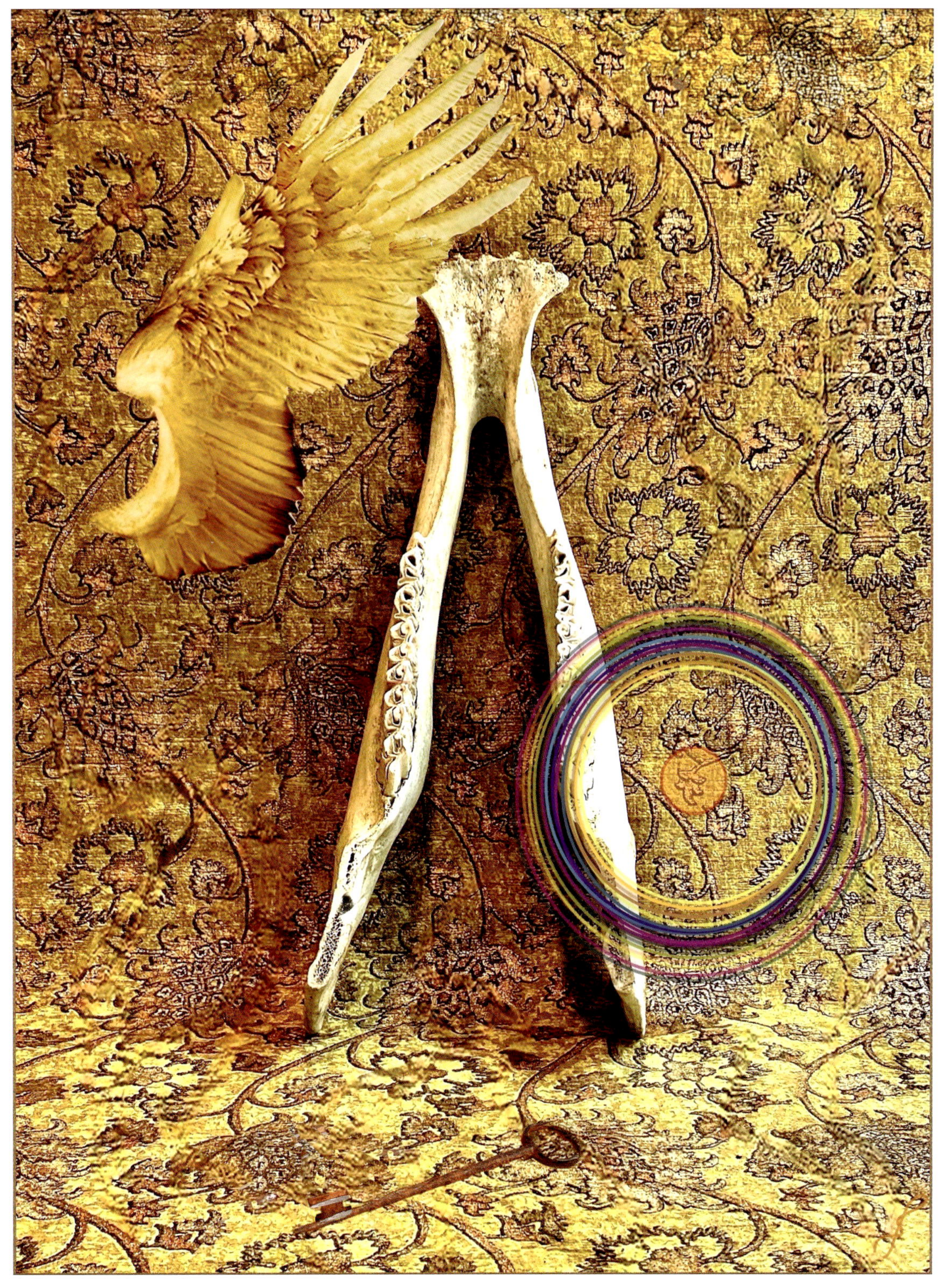

. . . and rings.

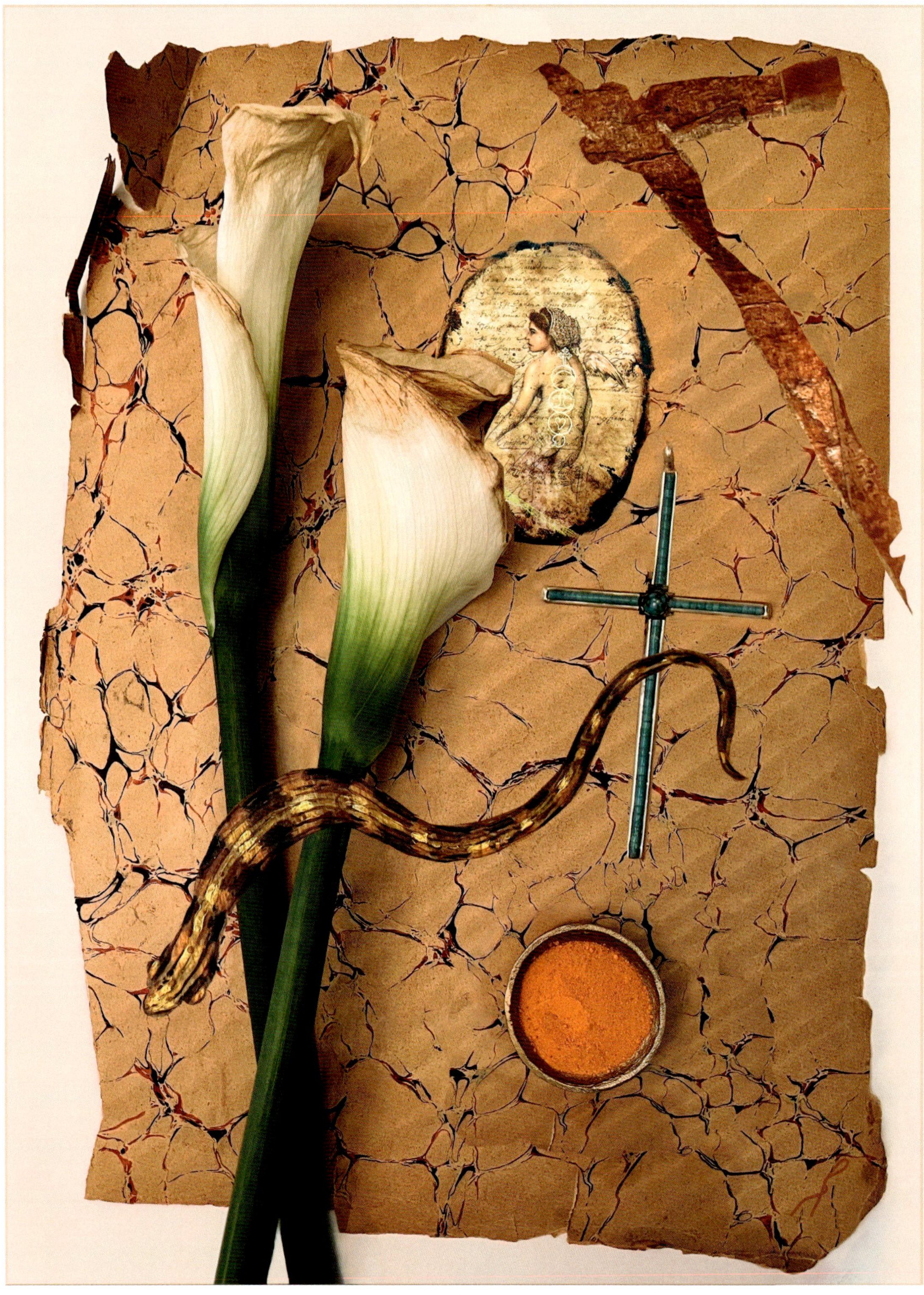

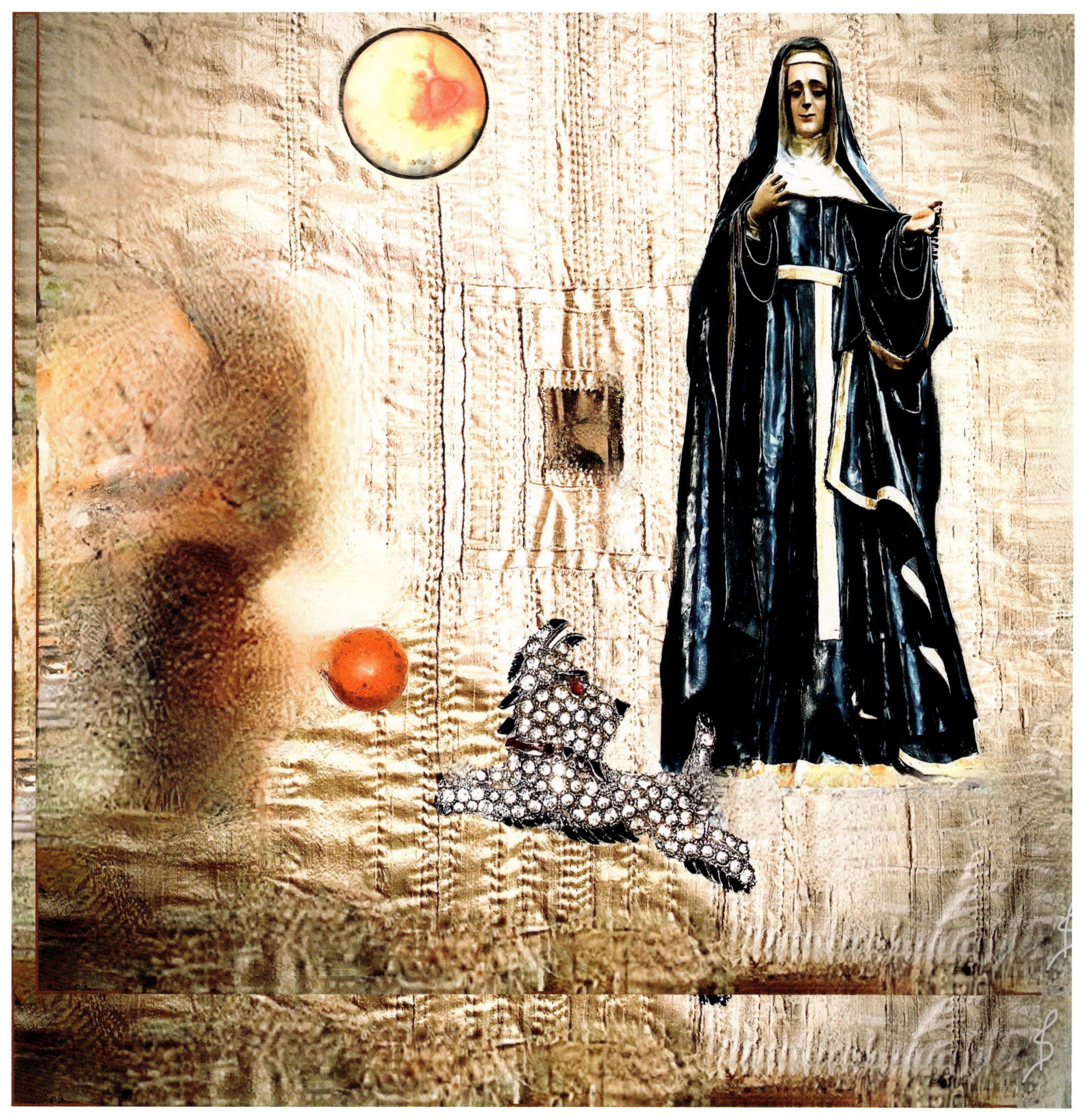

Symbols and secrets.

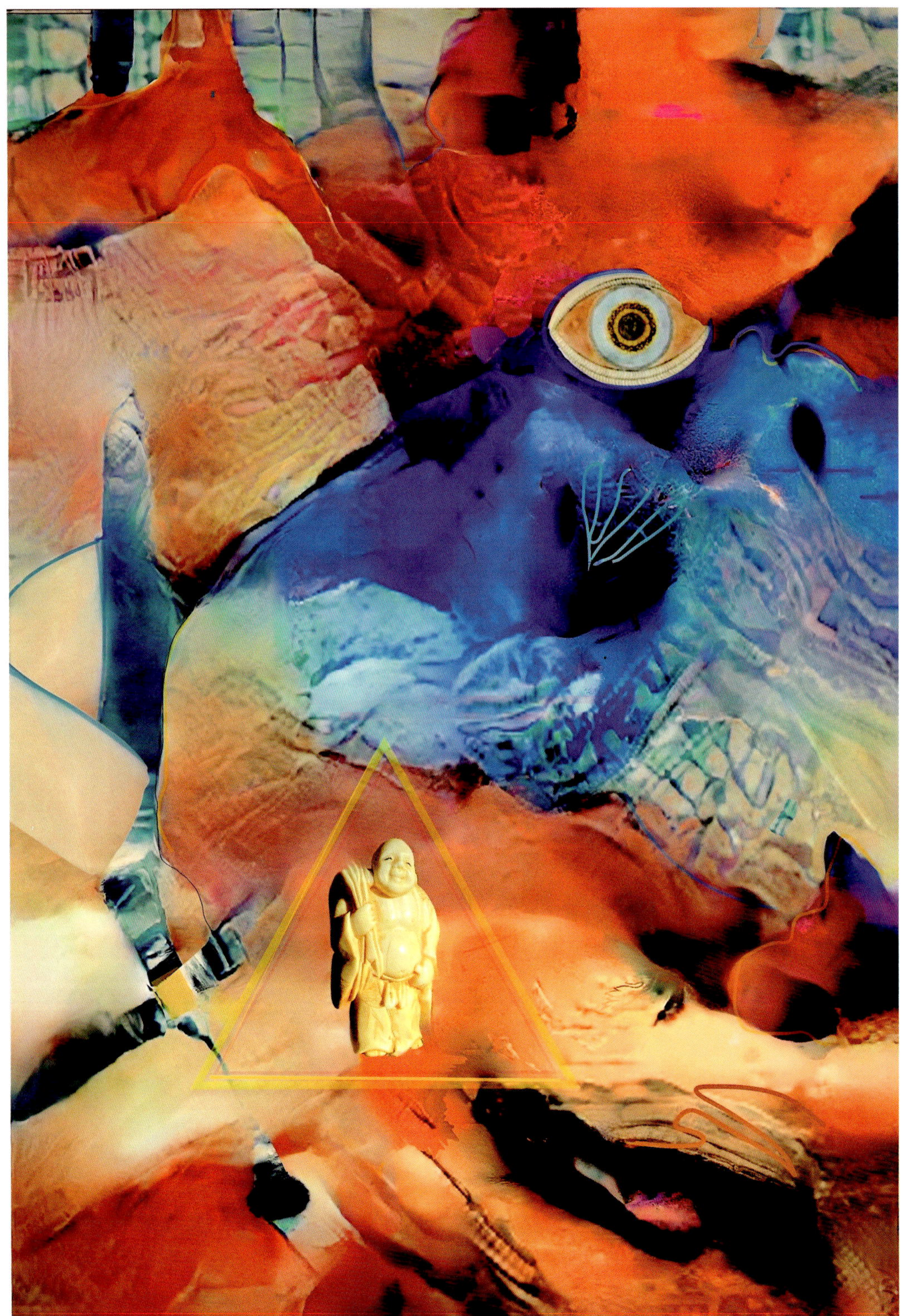

He sees, he laughs.

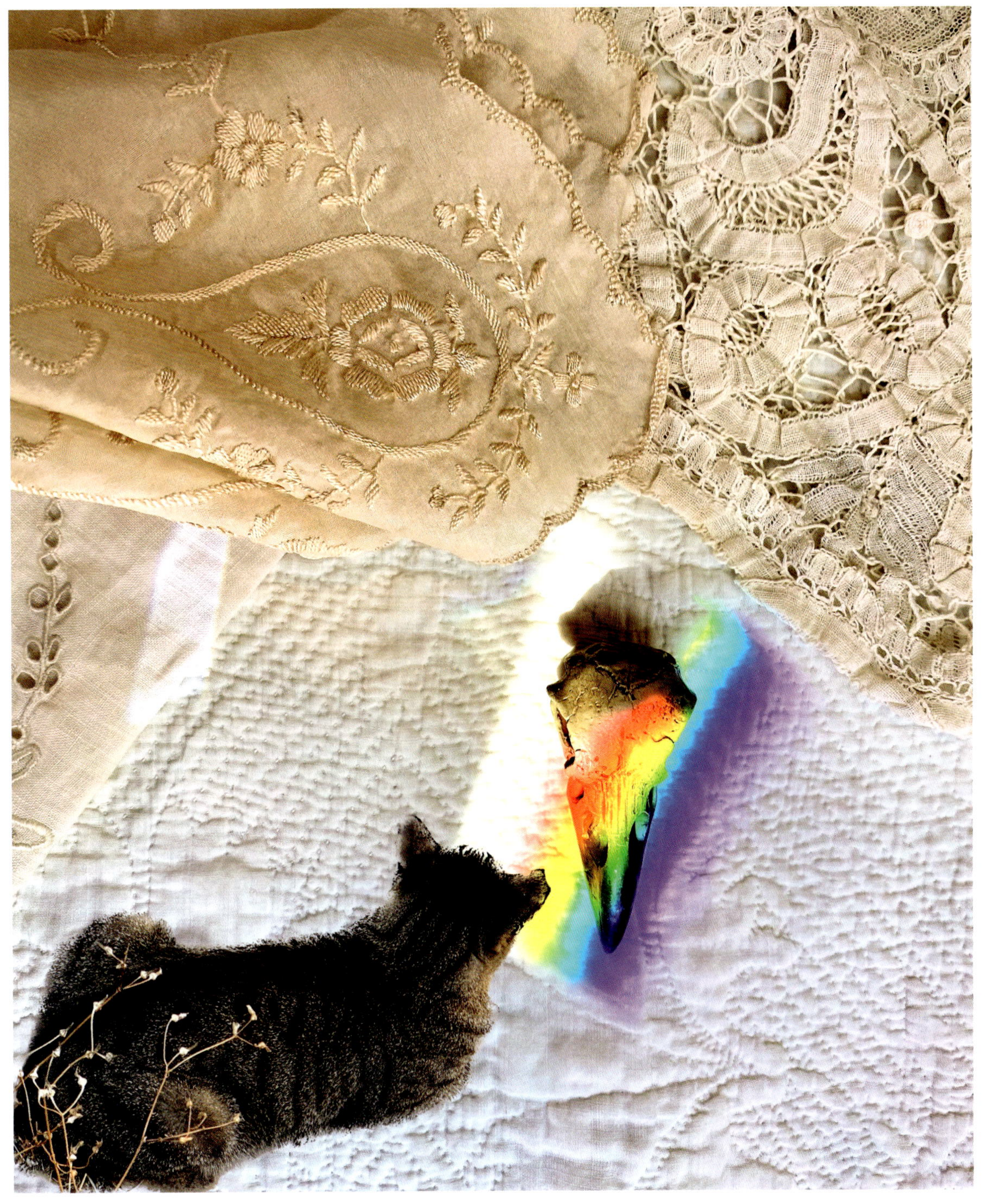

She ponders rainbows and bird skulls.

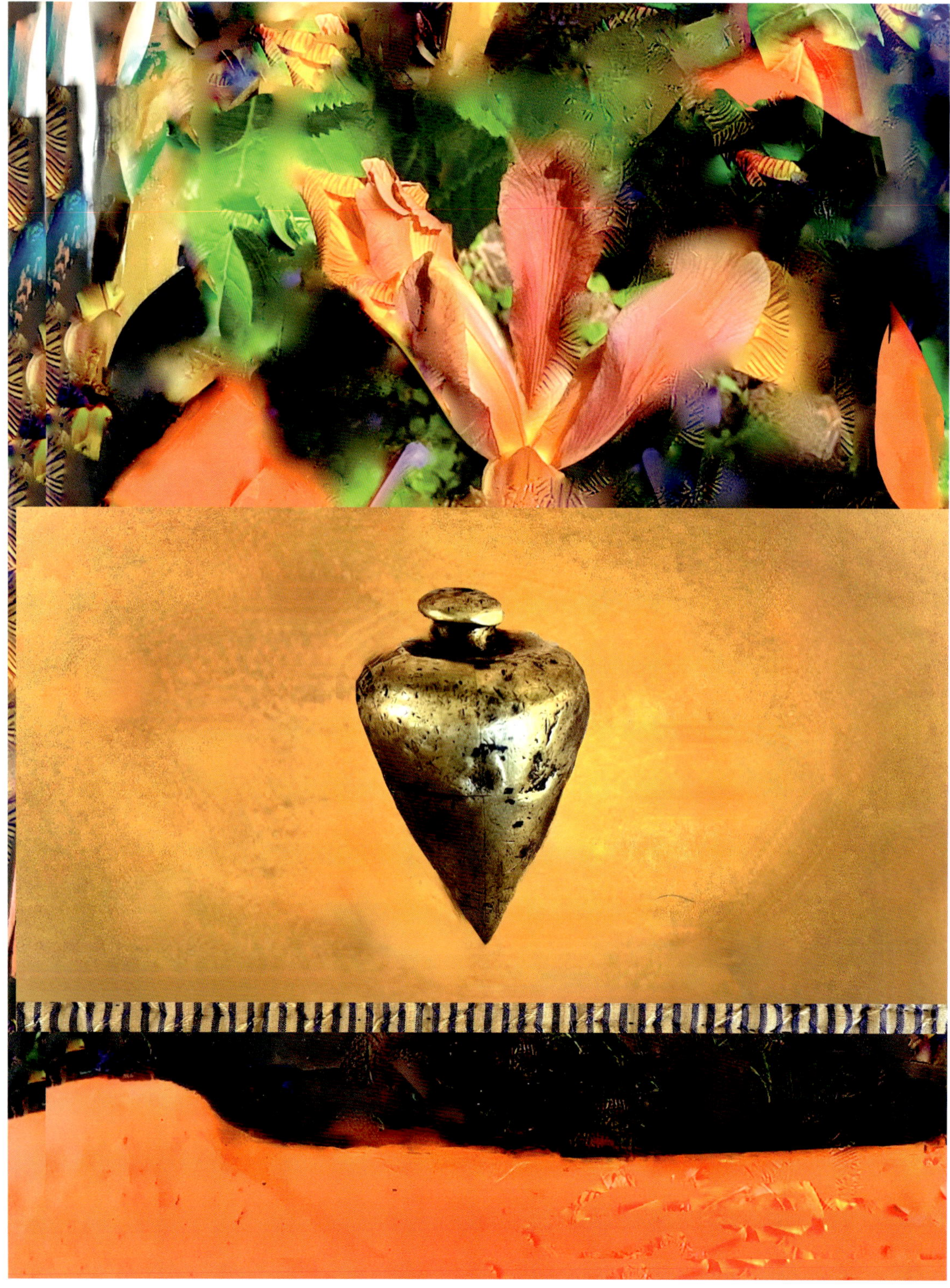

Coming through!

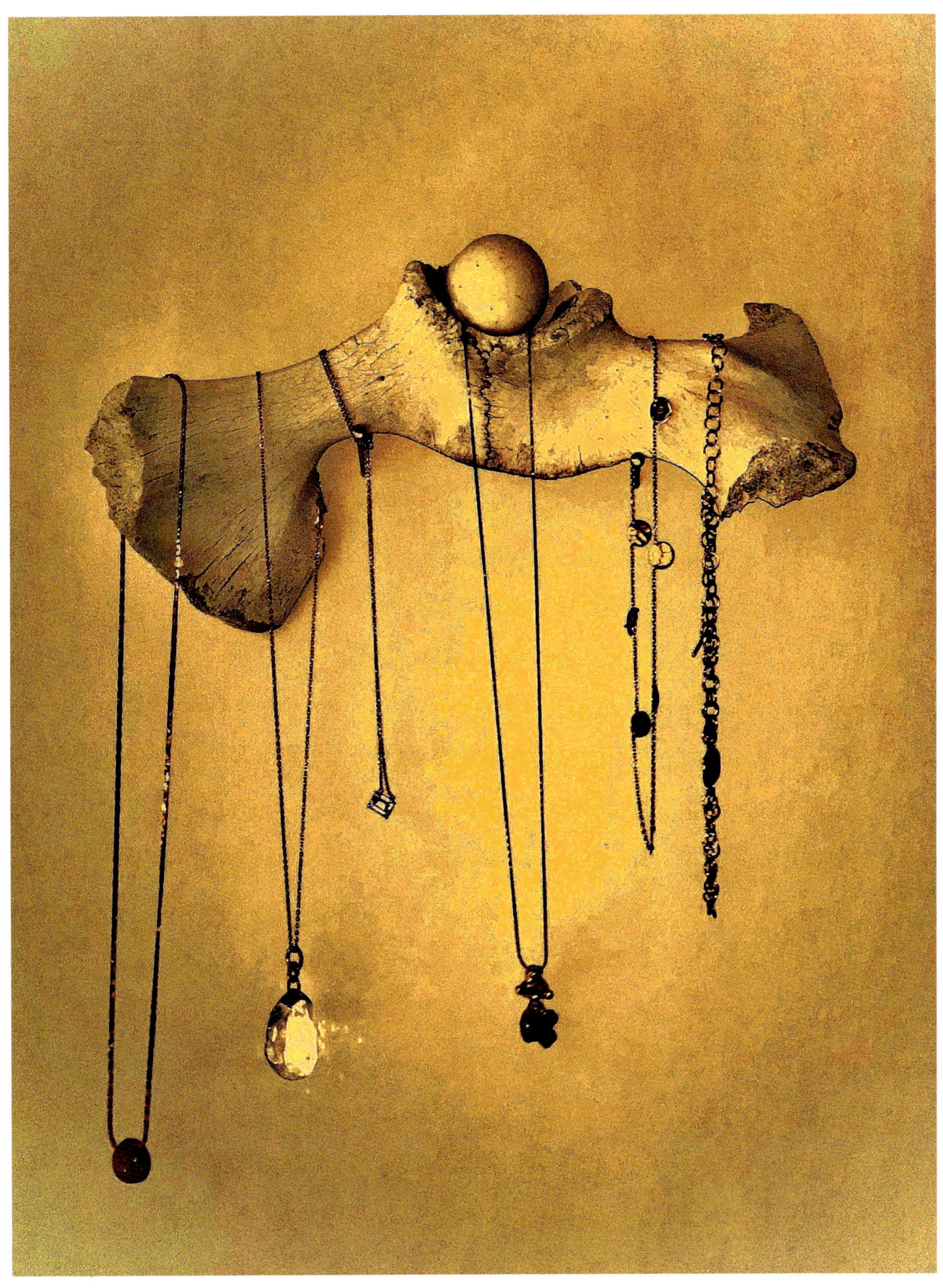

Gravity pulls apart and holds together.

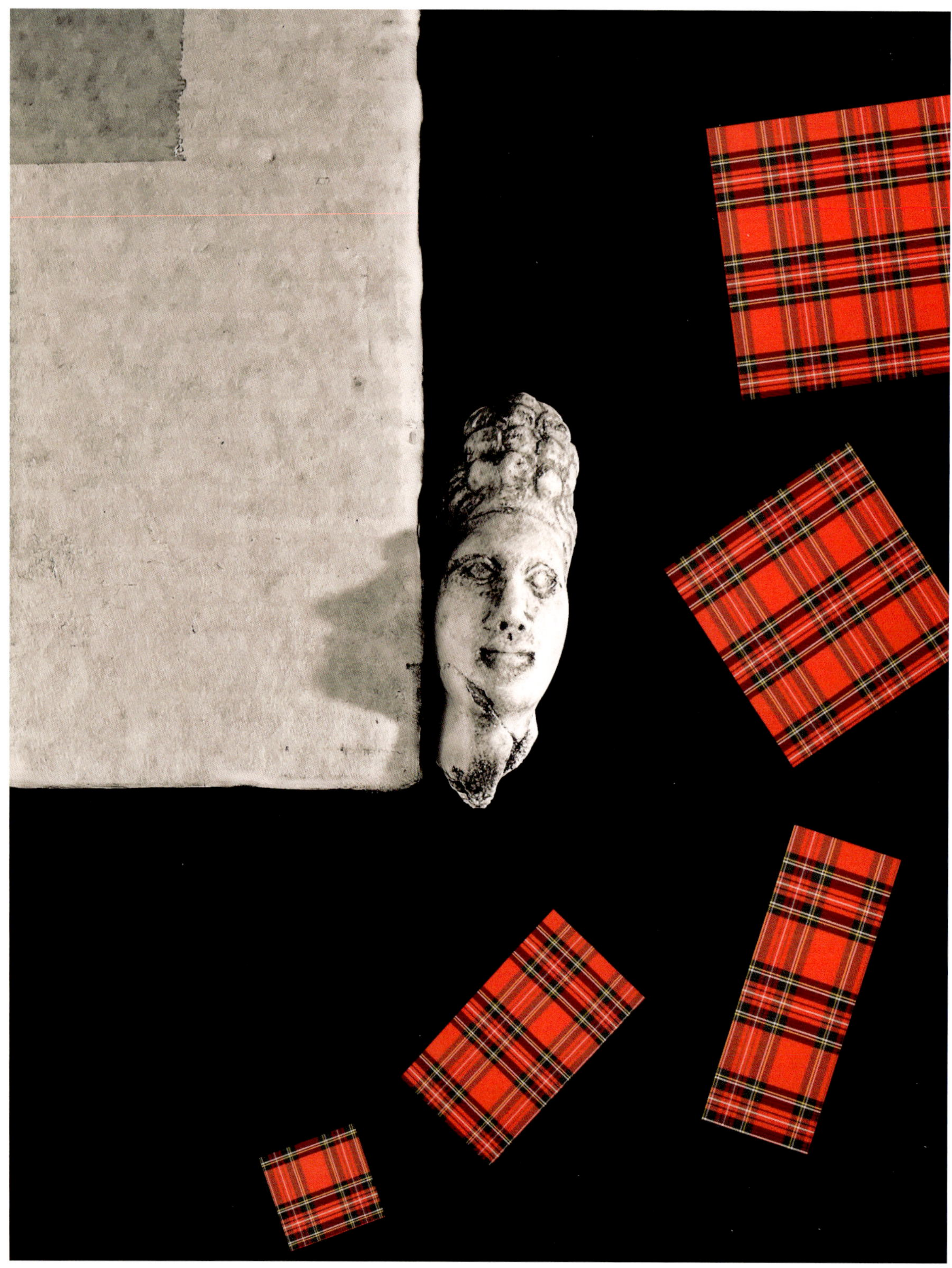

As soon as everyone leaves, she puts on her kilts!

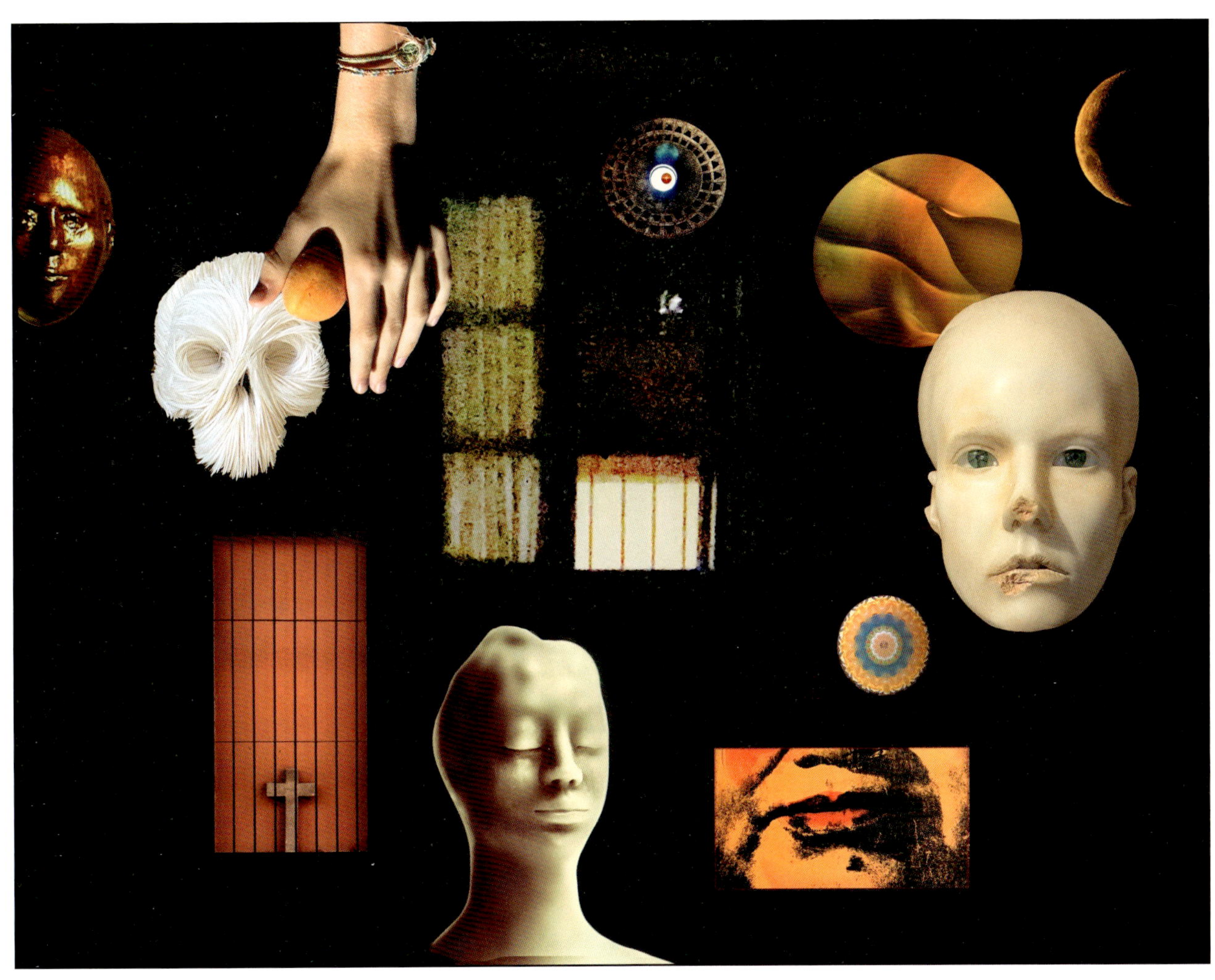

Mao & Friends is open for business.

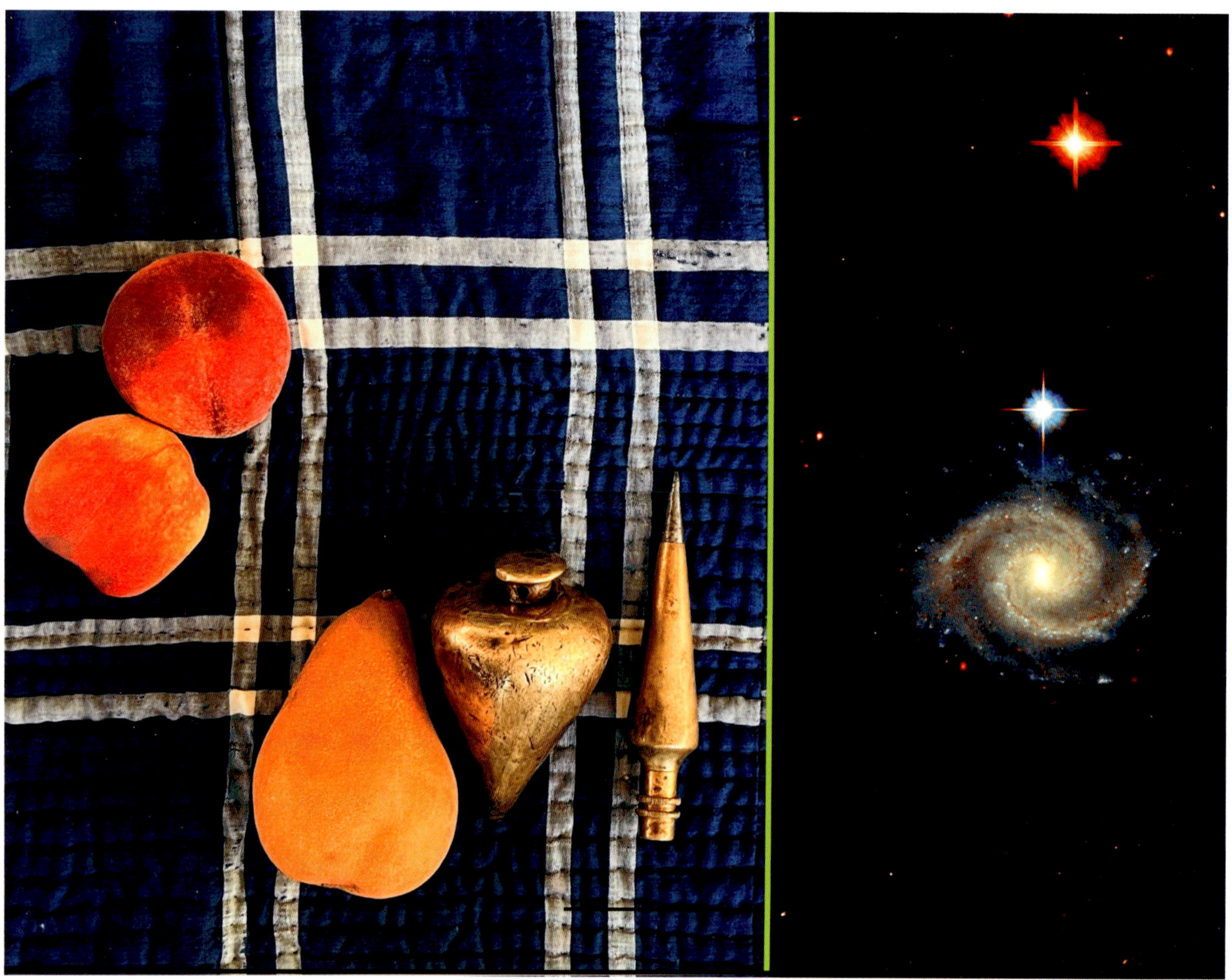

Wonders of the Universe.

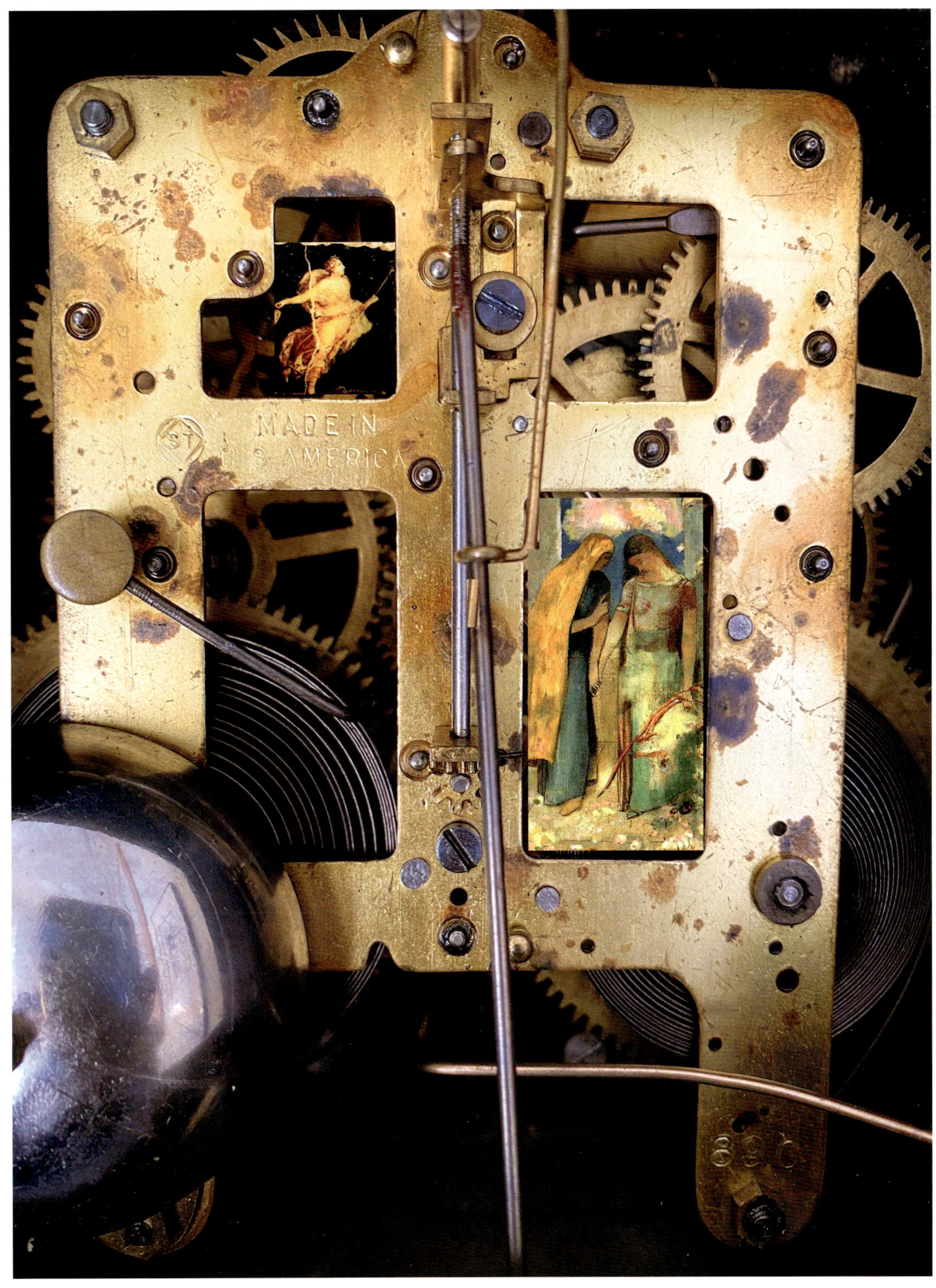

Tick tock, phantoms in the clock.

She could almost reach the key.

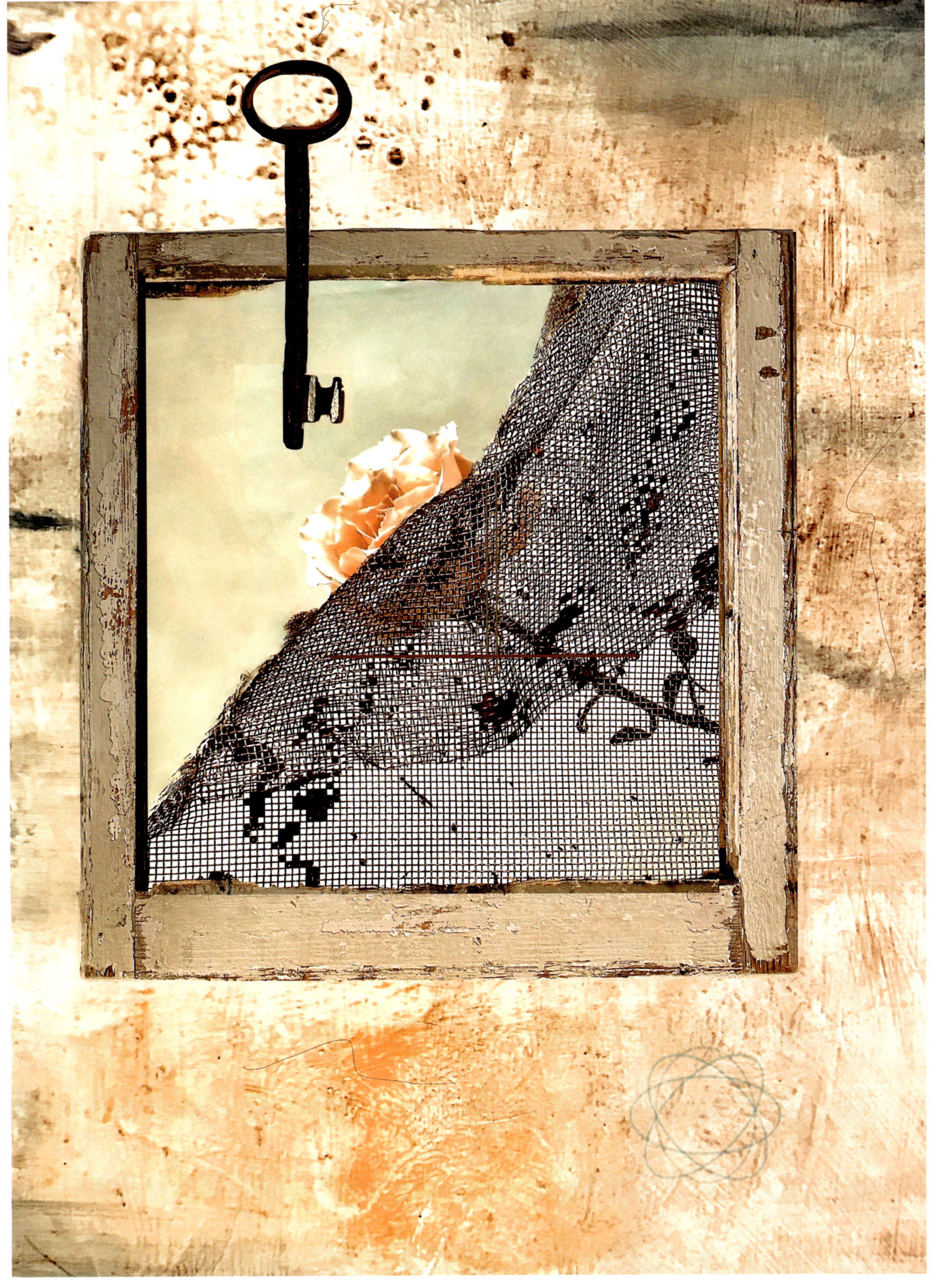

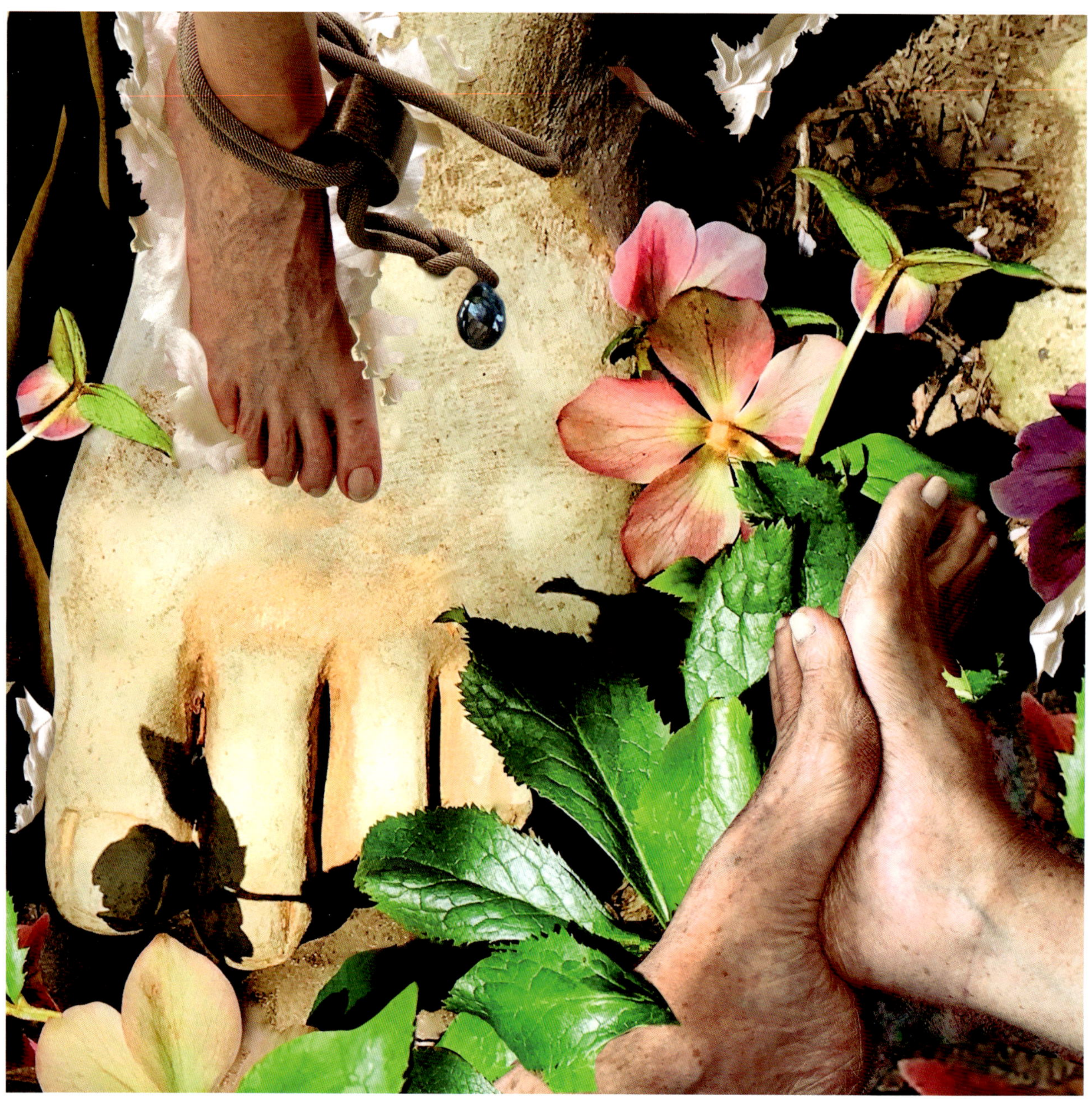

She locked him in among the flowers.

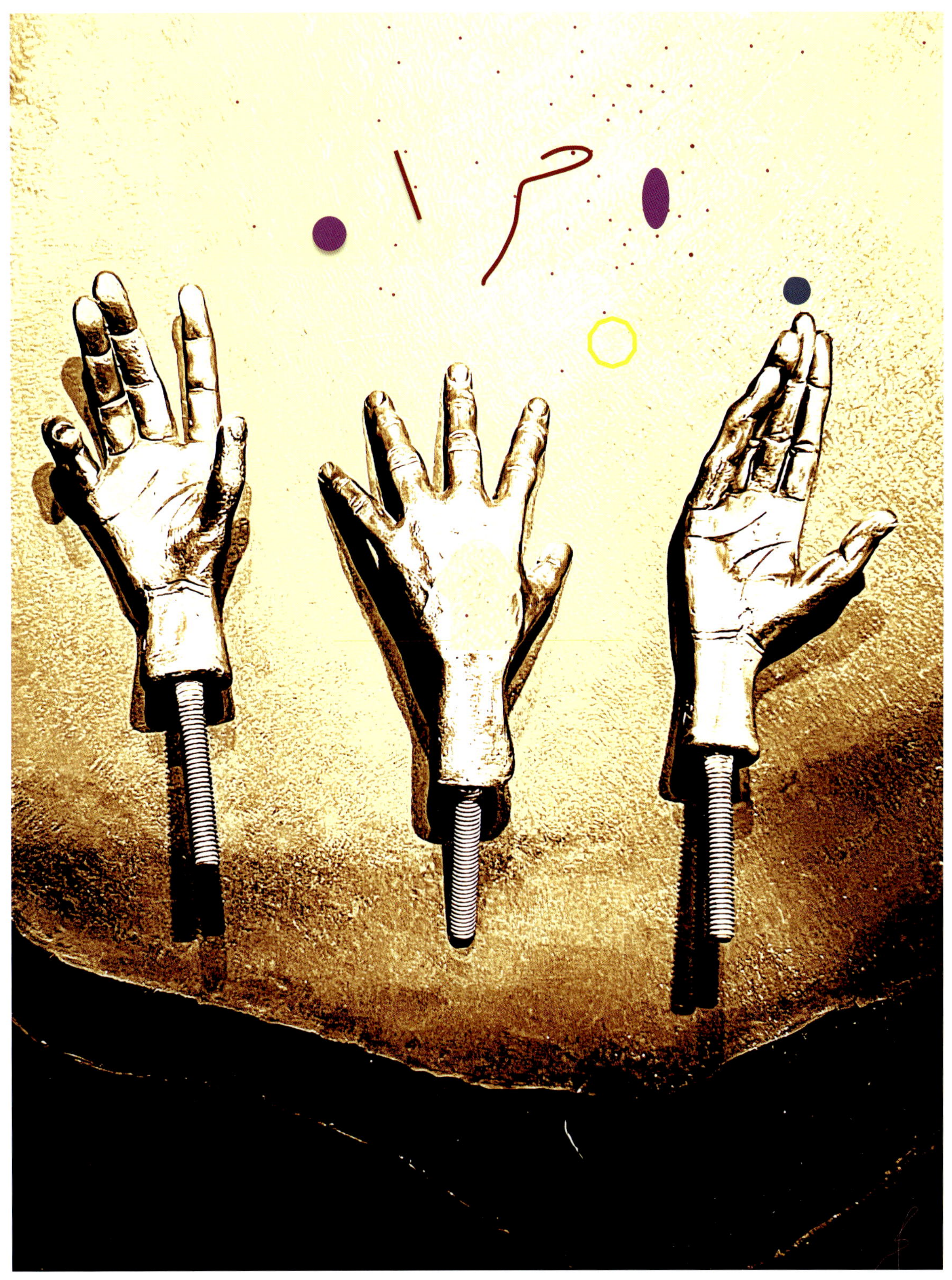

Struggling to become real.

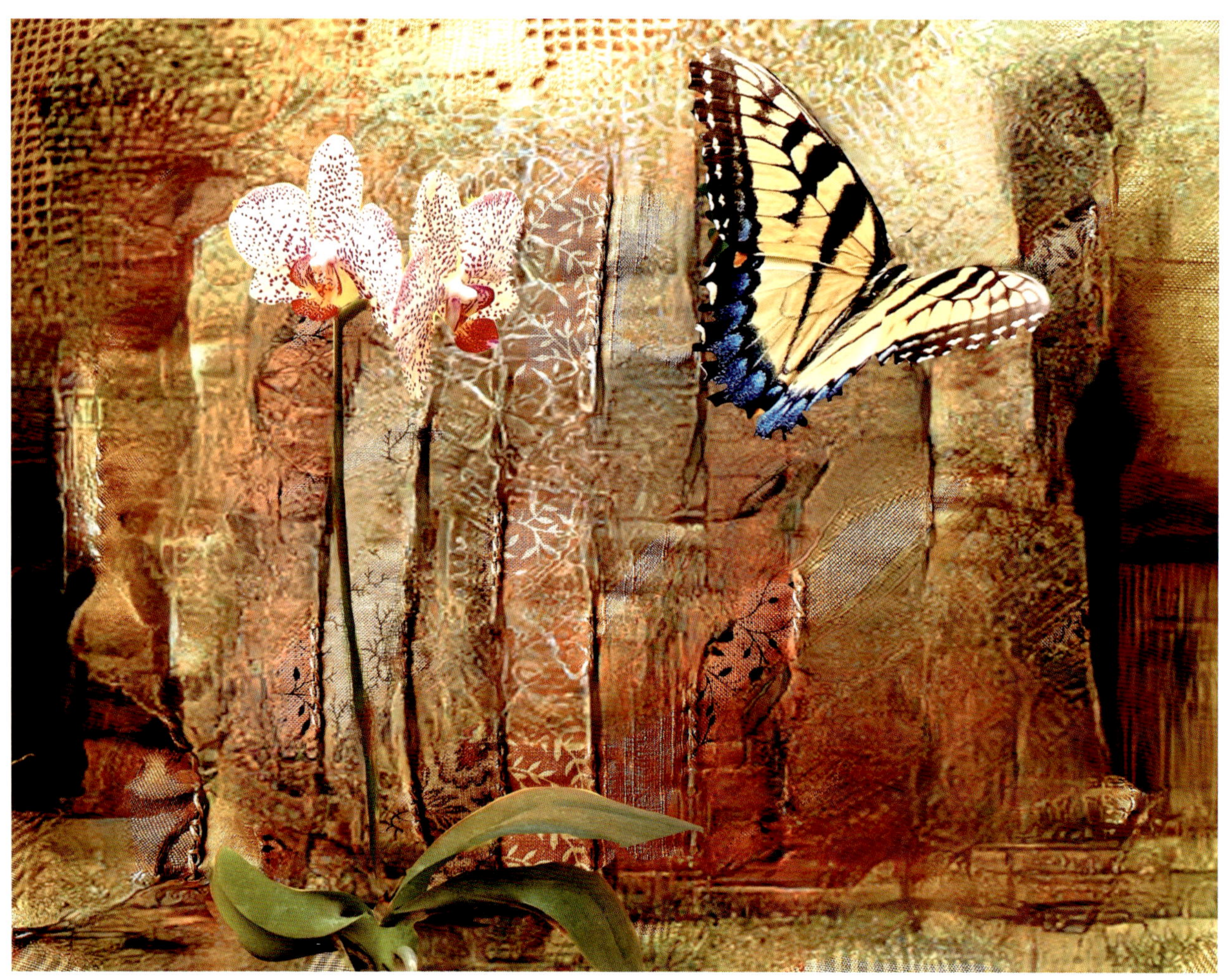

She started out in one piece . . .

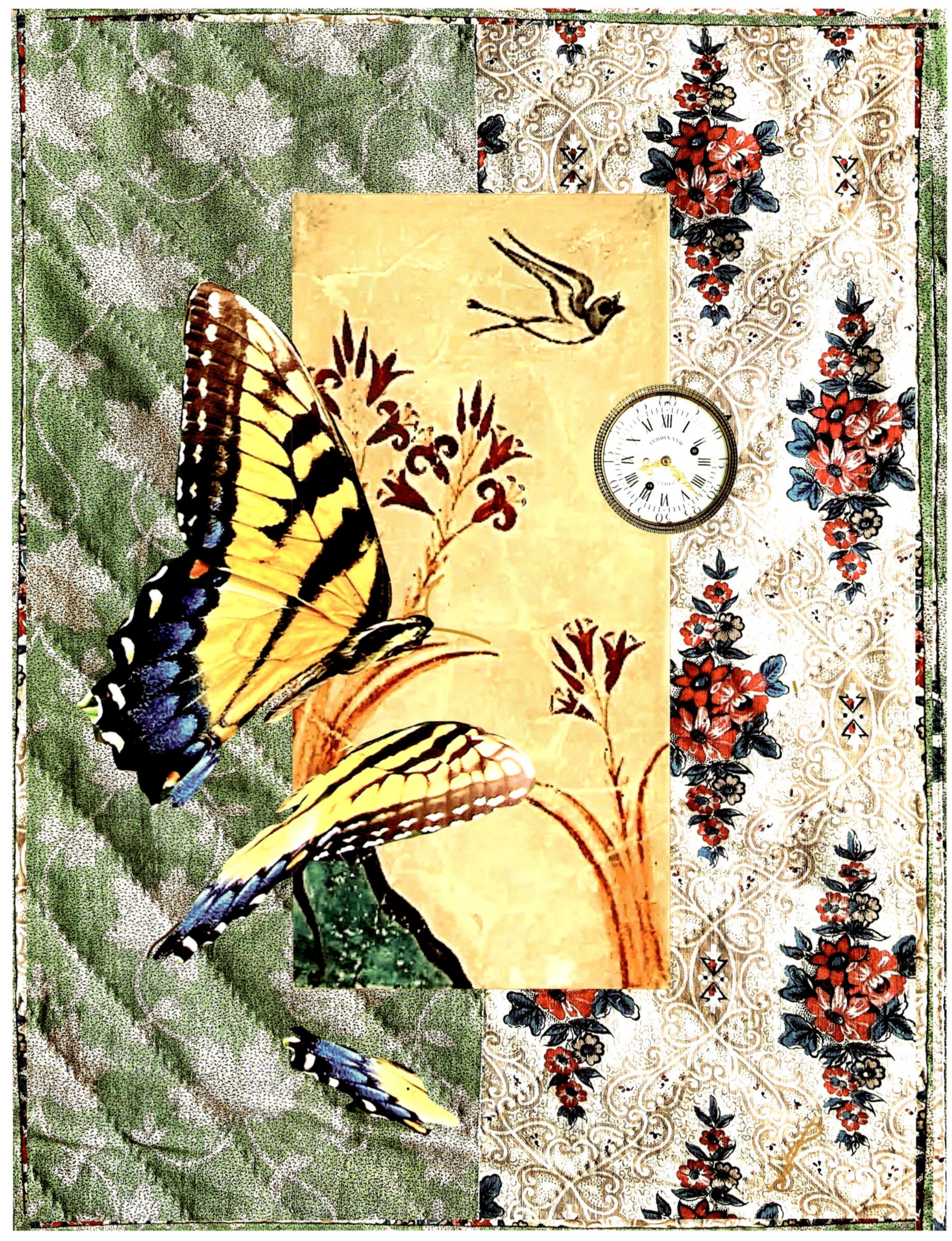

. . . but time and travel had an effect.

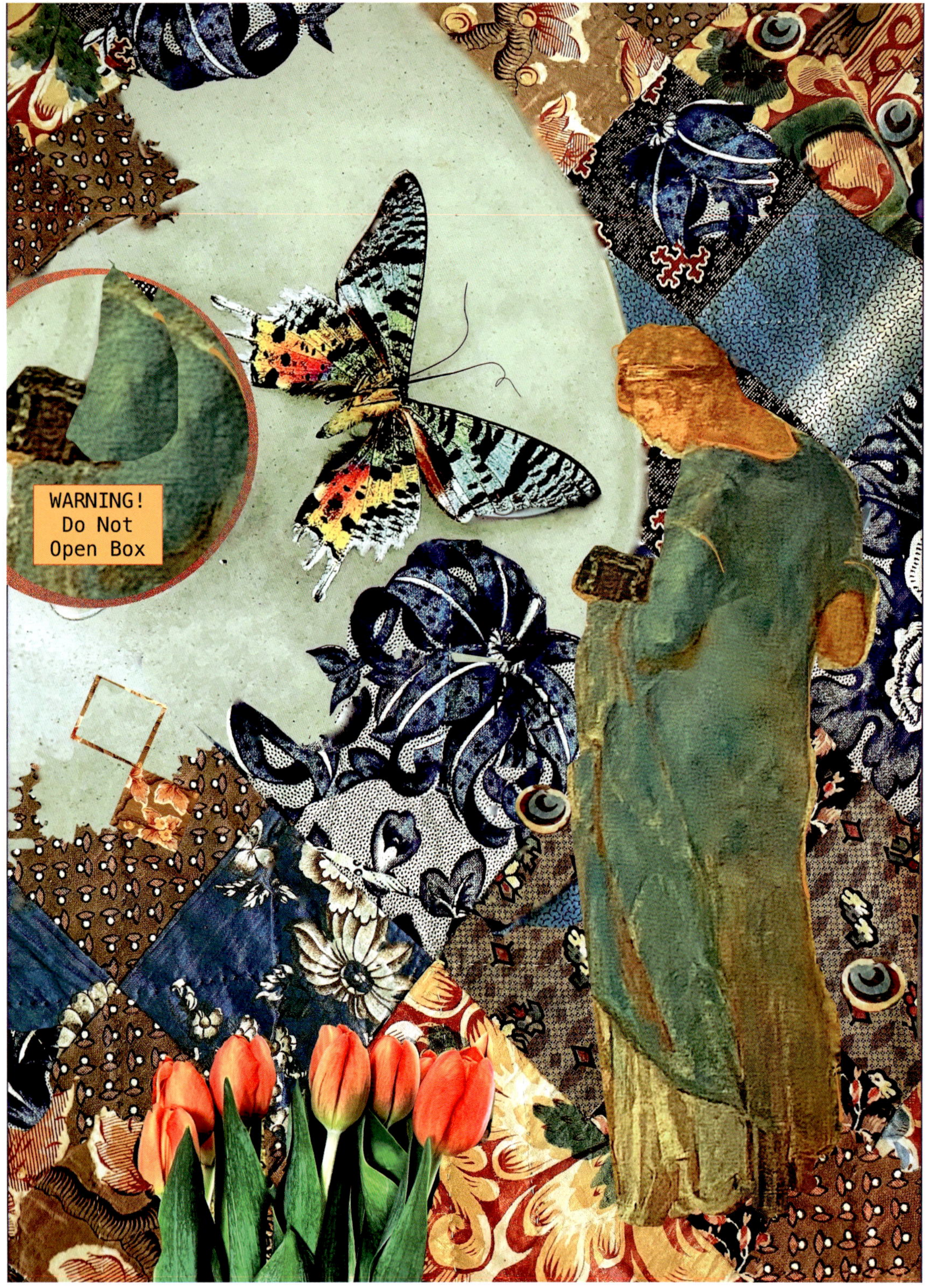

No! No! Stop! Do not open that box, Pandora.

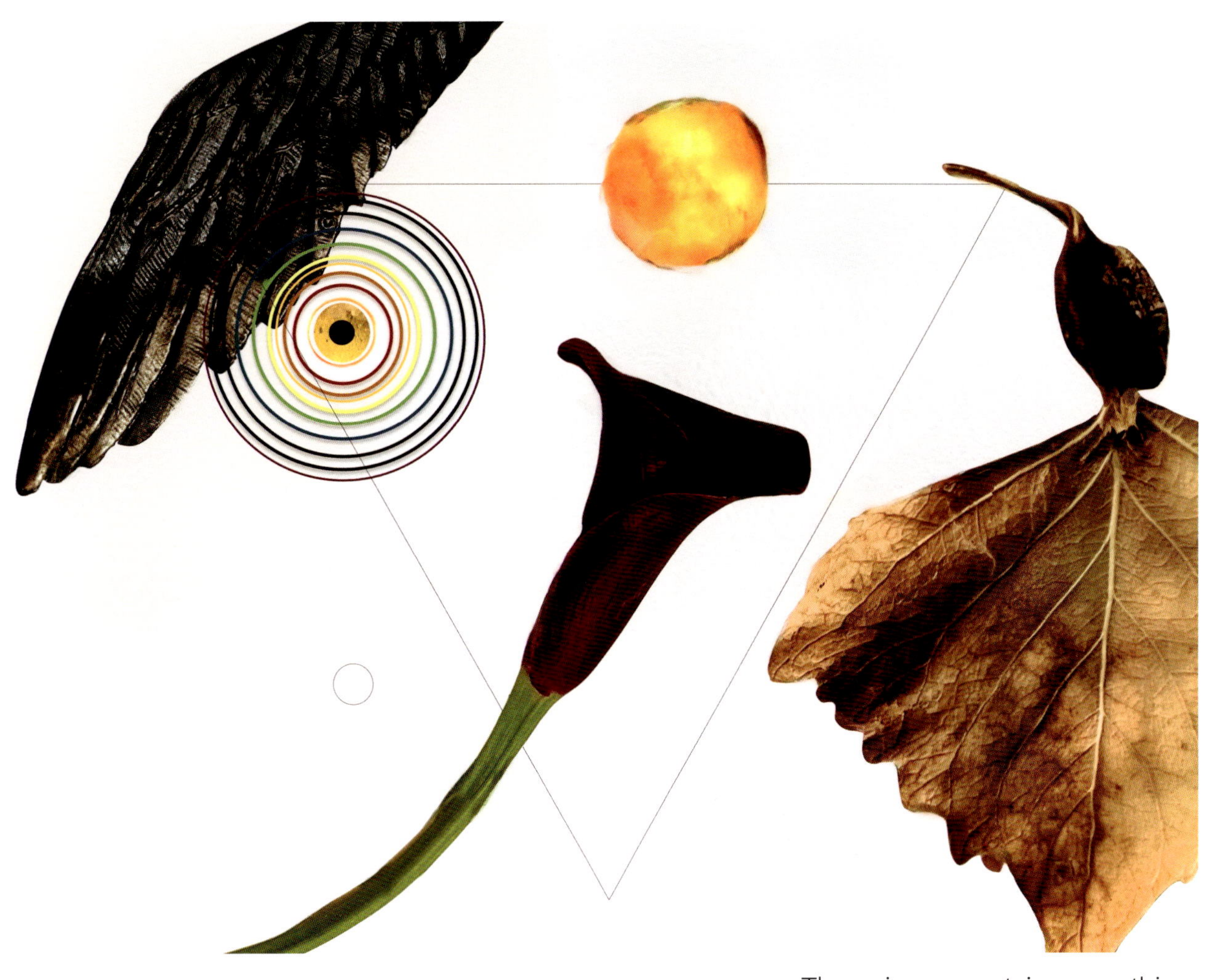

The universe contains everything.

Time and space create distance between us.

Memories and values weave tapestries—

warp and weft that cheat time and space of their tyranny.

PZS

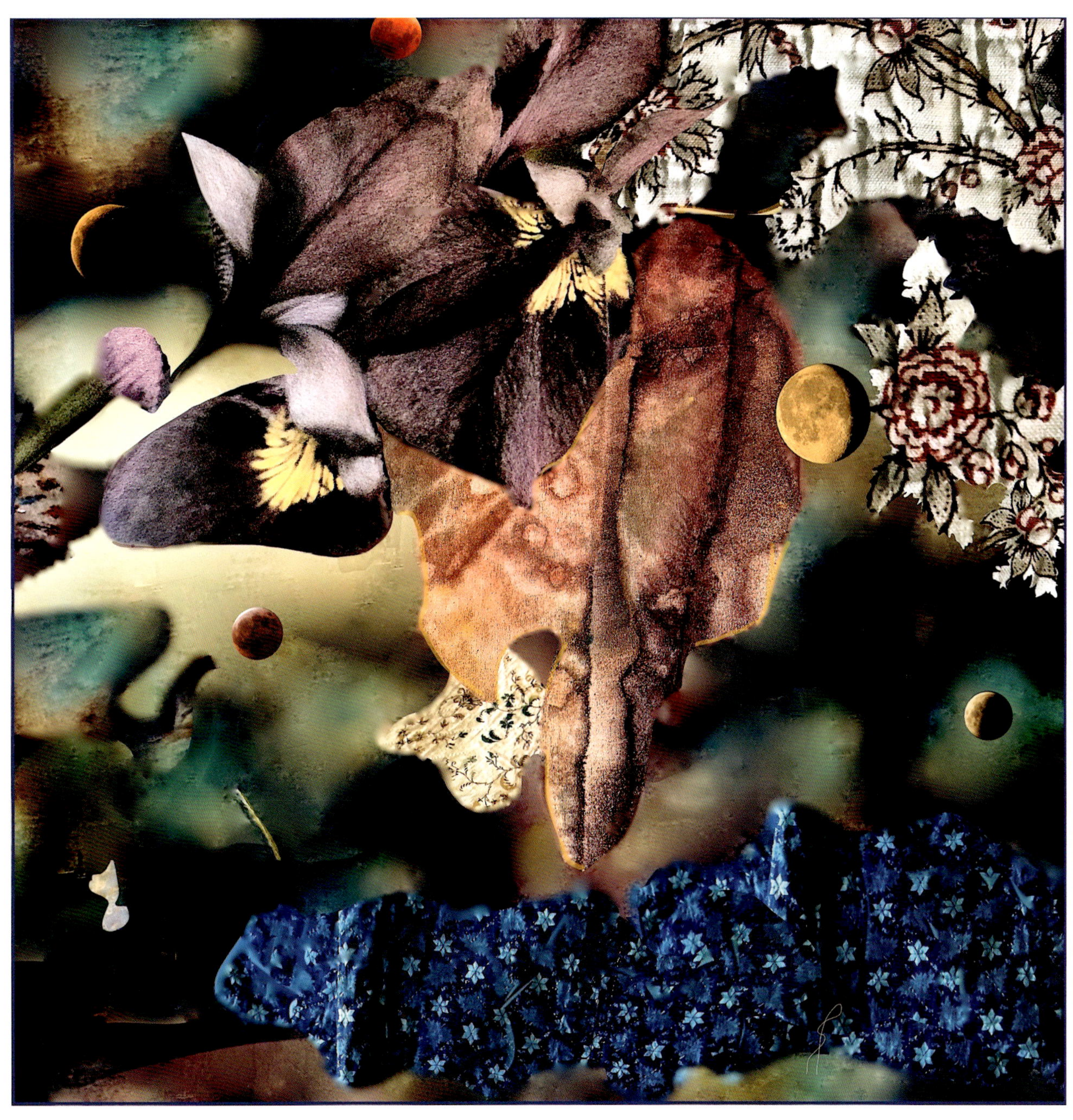

Moons tell time.

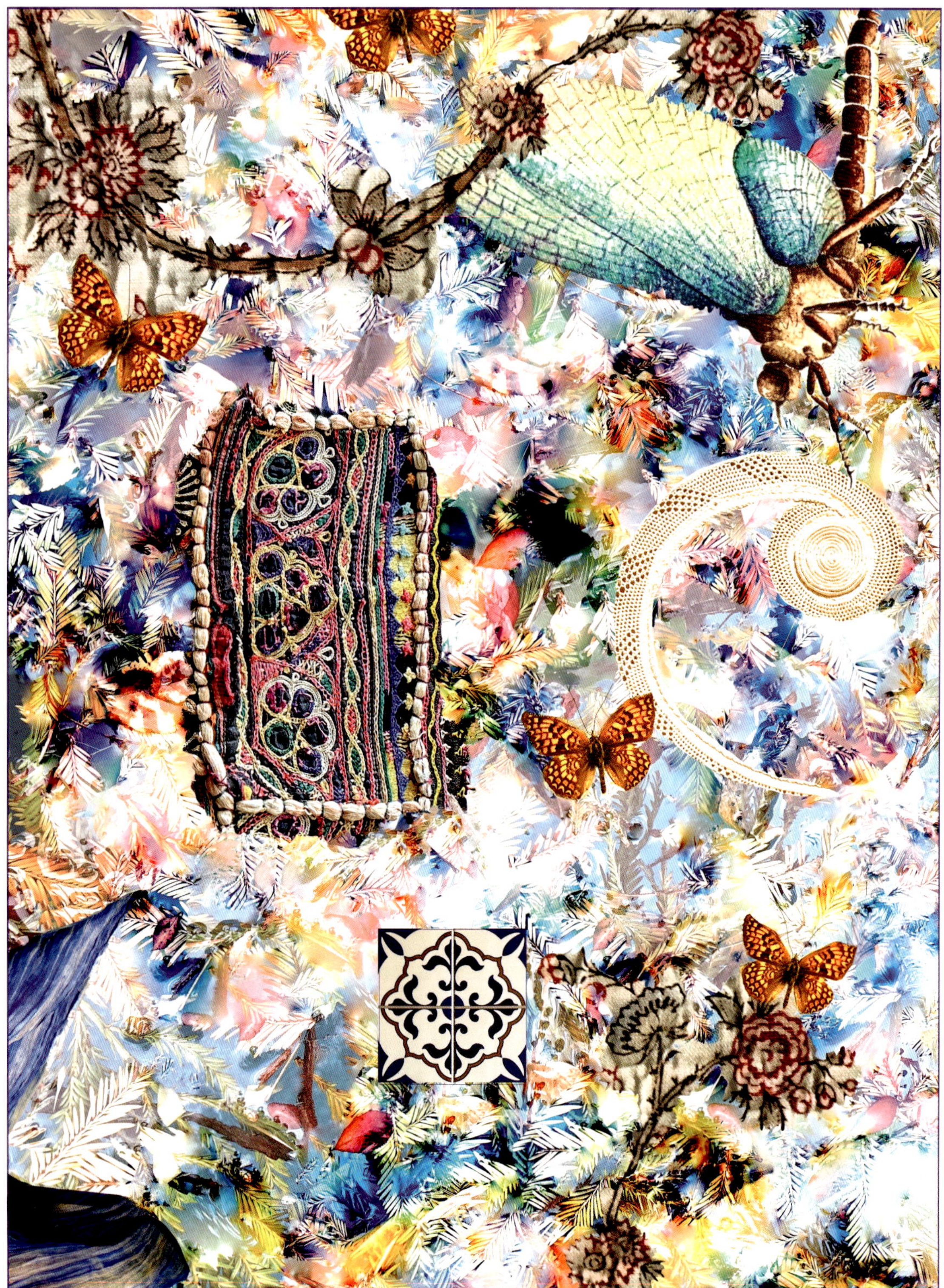

Space is filled with stories . . .

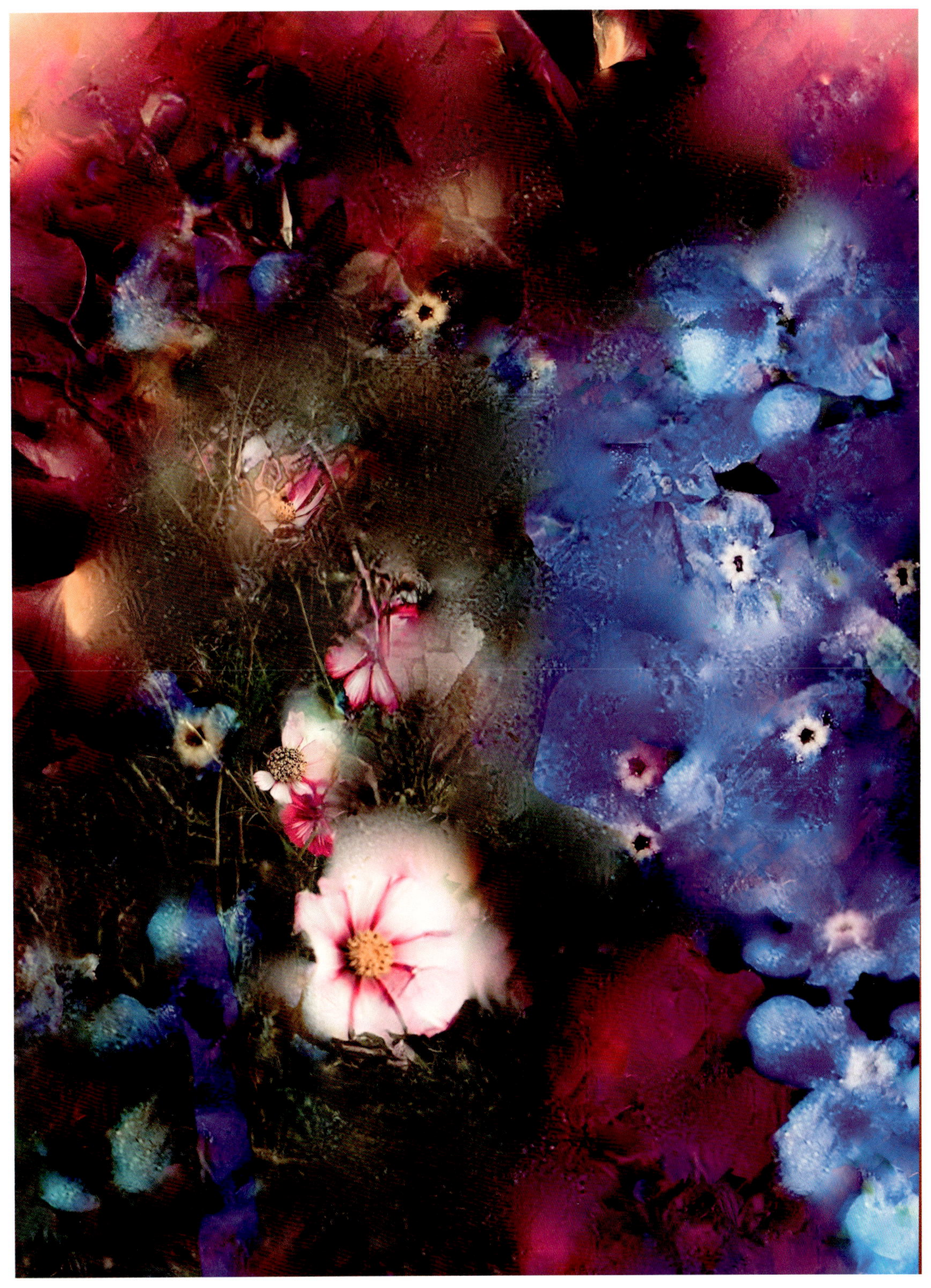

. . . and color.

Life is continually starting over.

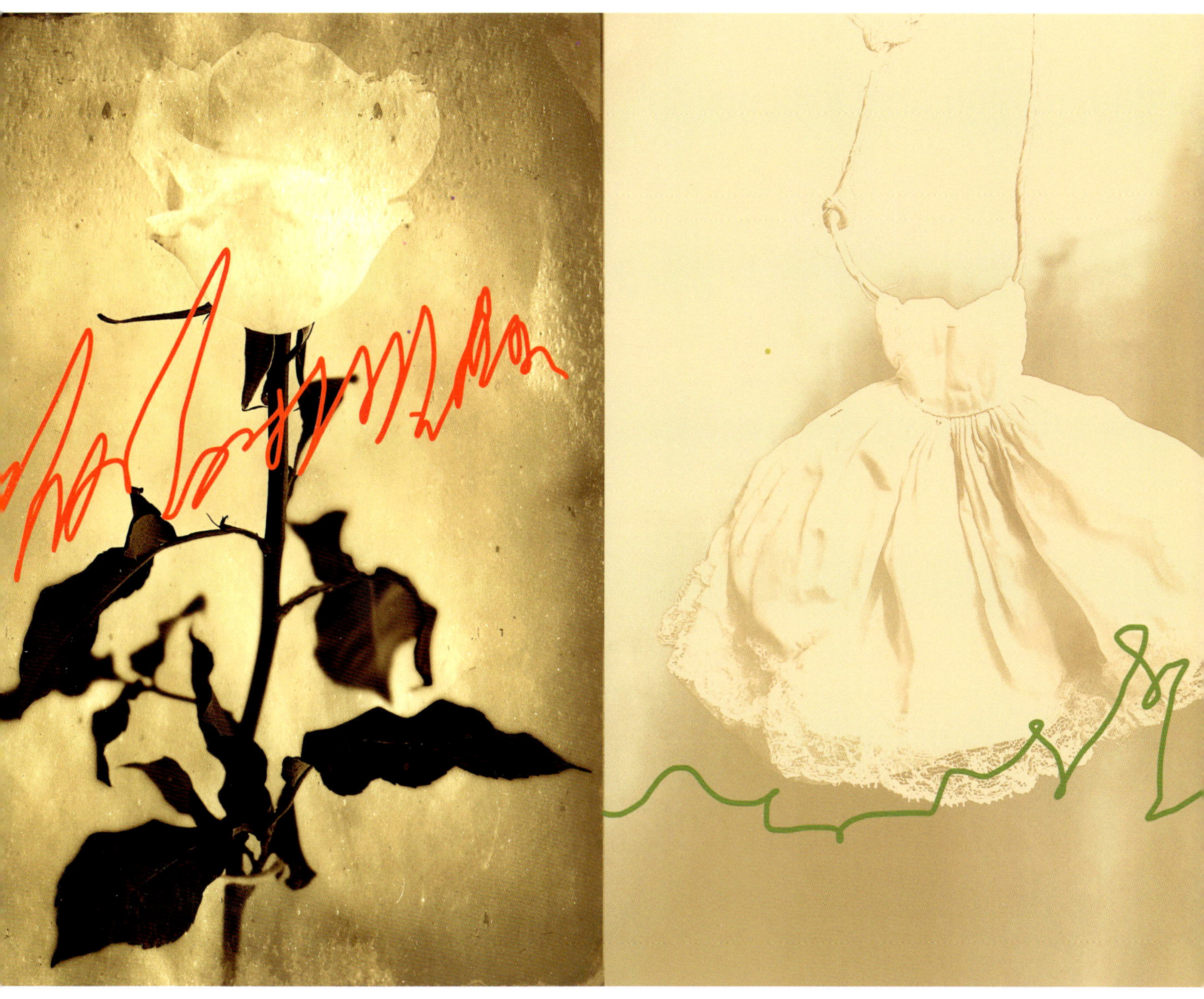

GODOT and a TURTLE

(A Large Tortoise and a Turtle are by a Tree.)

TORTOISE
His name is Godot, that's what they call him.

TURTLE
And humans just wait for him?

TORTOISE
Yes.

TURTLE
Anxiously?

TORTOISE
Sometimes.

TURTLE
Why are they waiting?

TORTOISE
I don't know.

TURTLE
What is waiting?

TORTOISE
It's stopping a part of yourself, expecting something to happen.

(The TORTOISE sighs, slowly)

a n d　　a　　T O R T O I S E

TURTLE
Isn't something happening right now?

(TURTLE doesn't even move.)

TORTOISE
Absolutely.

(TURTLE and TORTOISE look out.
 It's quiet. Still. They don't move.)

TORTOISE
I feel so alive.

TURTLE
Me too.

(TURTLE and TORTOISE sit very still.)

TURTLE
What's the difference between waiting and living?

(A very long pause)

TORTOISE
Everything.

(not) The End

Play for *Forever* by KAREN ZACARIAS
Playwright, 2021 US Artist Fellow. Plays include *Sins of Sor Juana*,
Native Gardens, Destiny of Desire, The Book Club Play, Legacy of Light

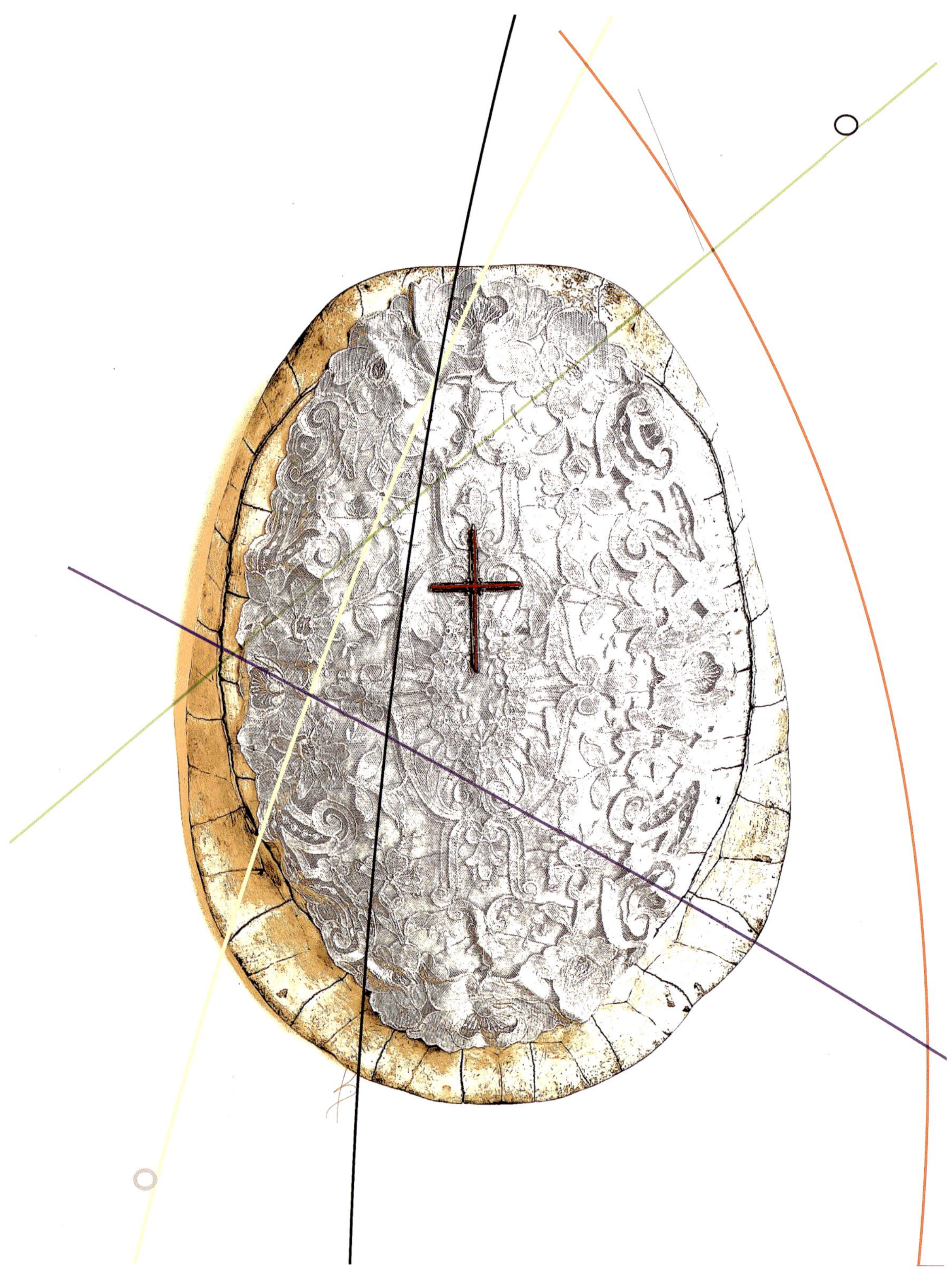

Gramma left her best lace to me.

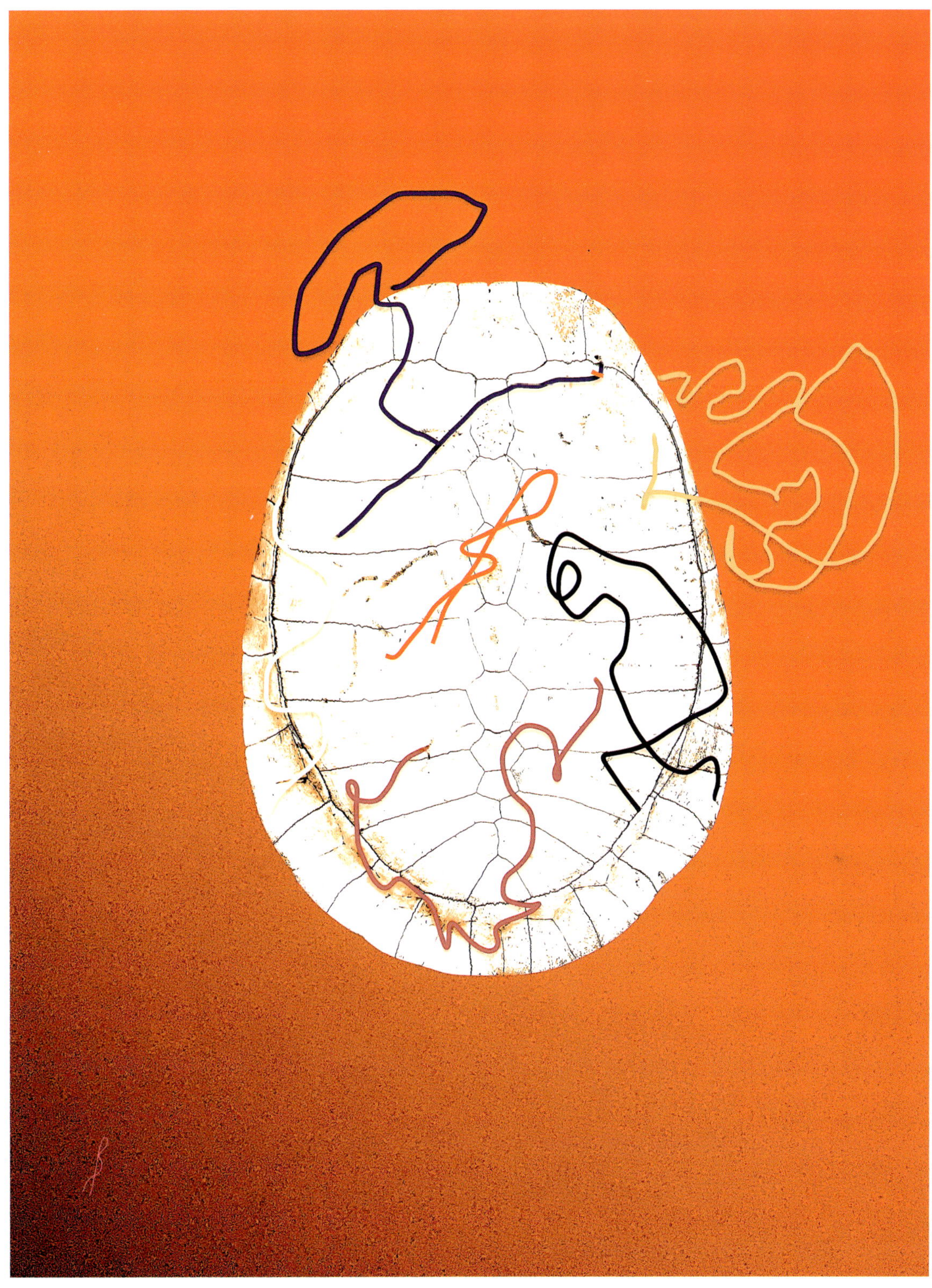

I'm hanging on by a thread.

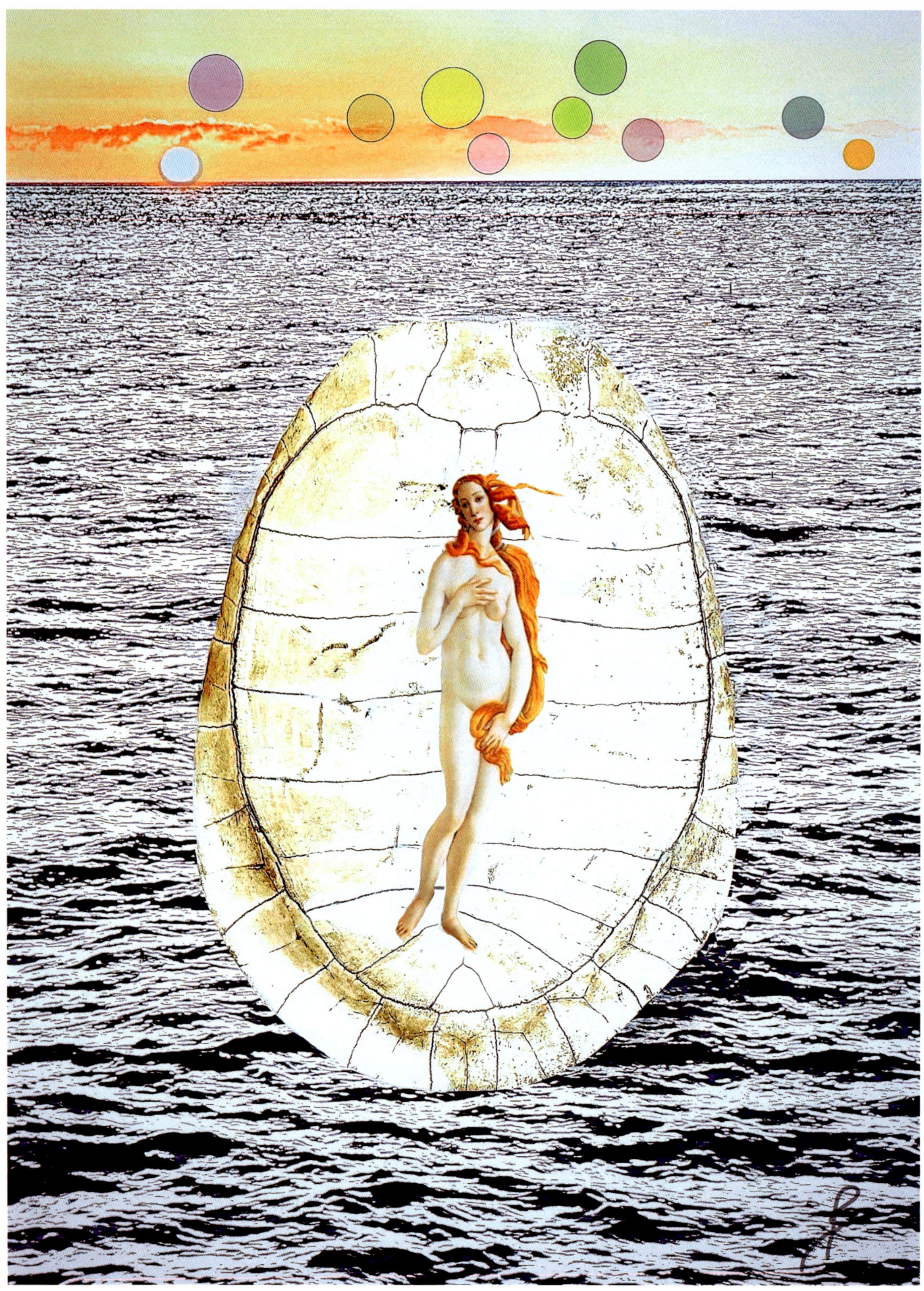

"She was a good swimmer, too."

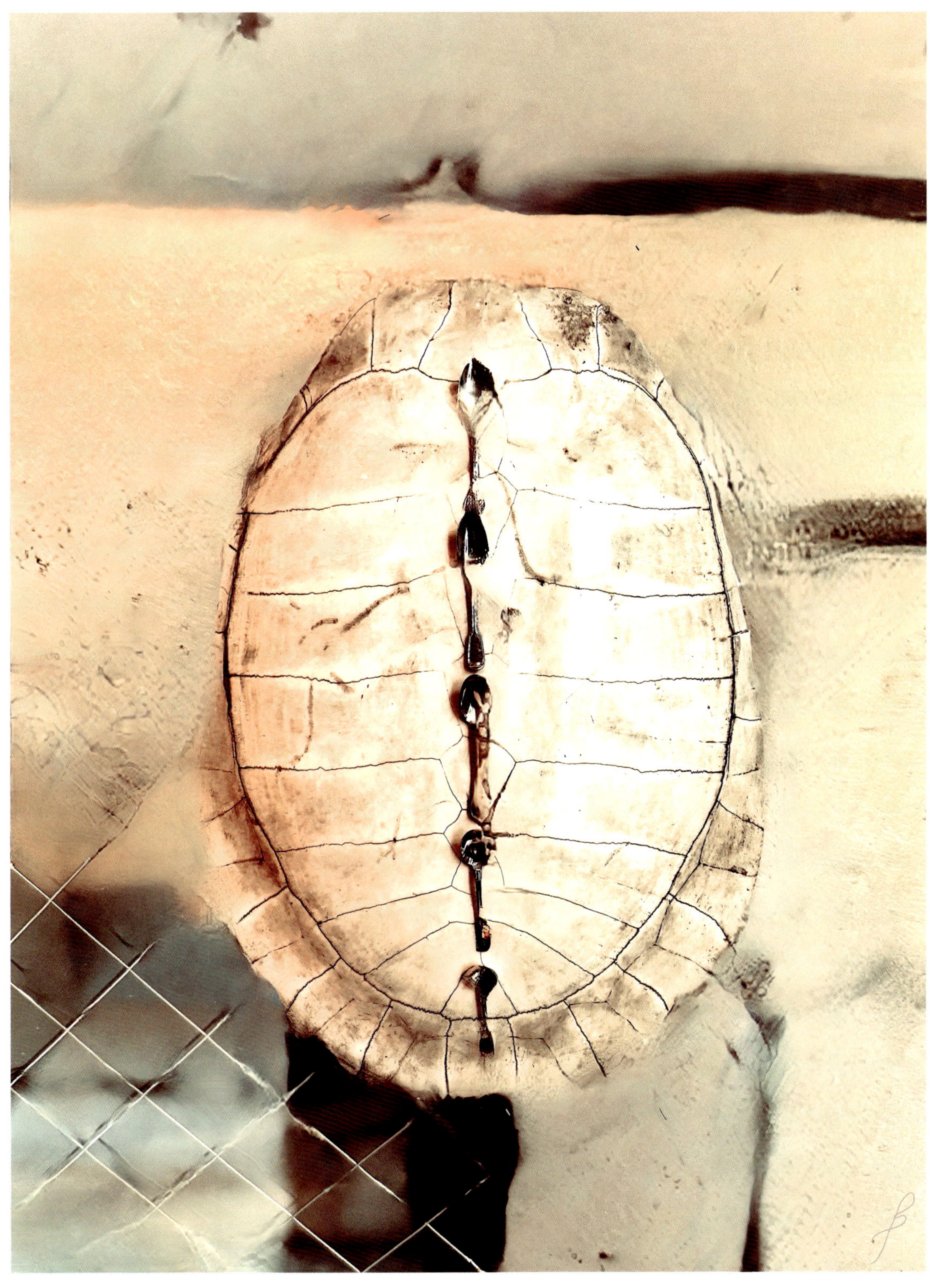

After the Titanic sank, I started my collection of spoons.

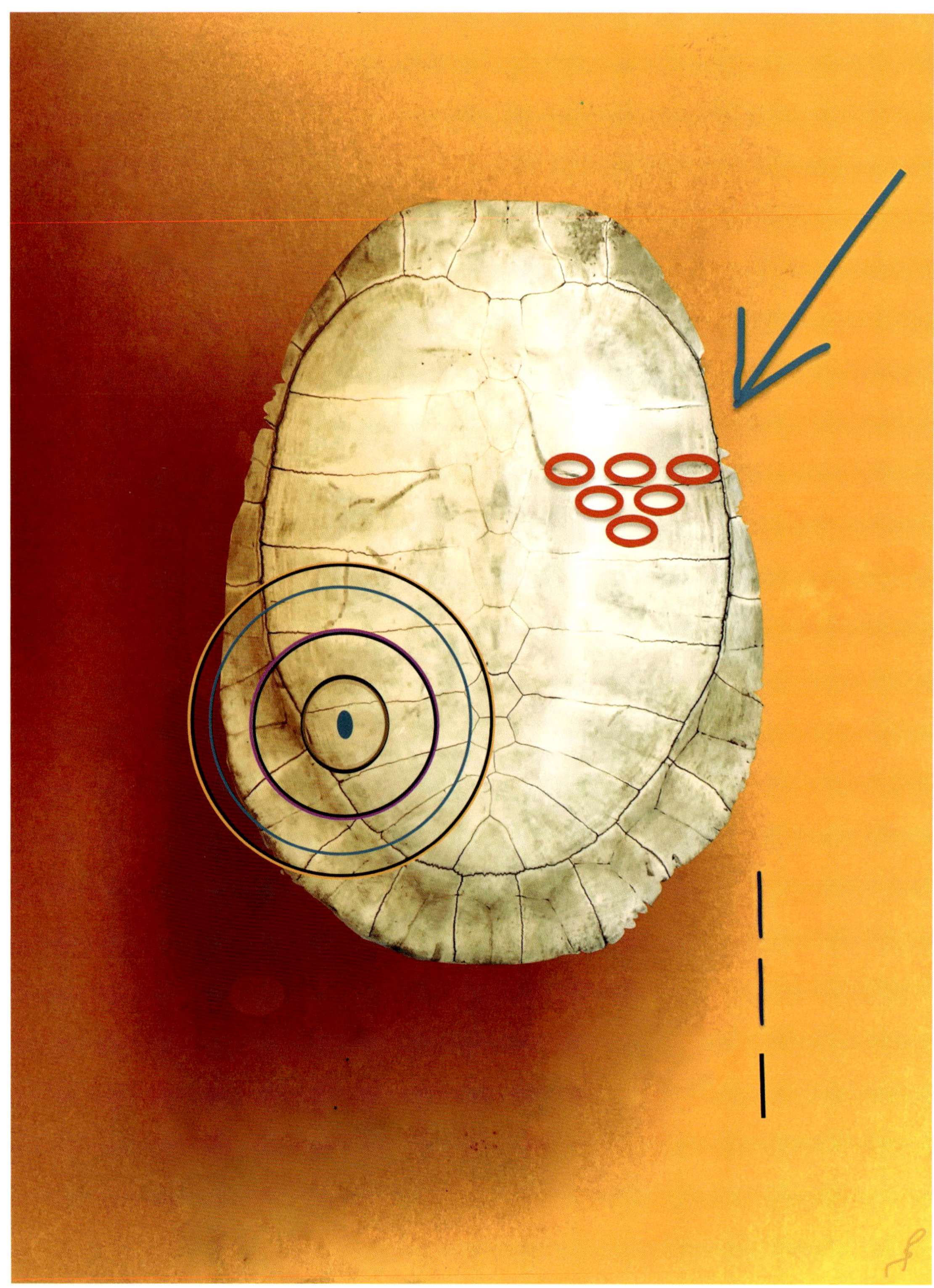

"Great Uncle Joe painted these directions on my back so I'd never be lost."

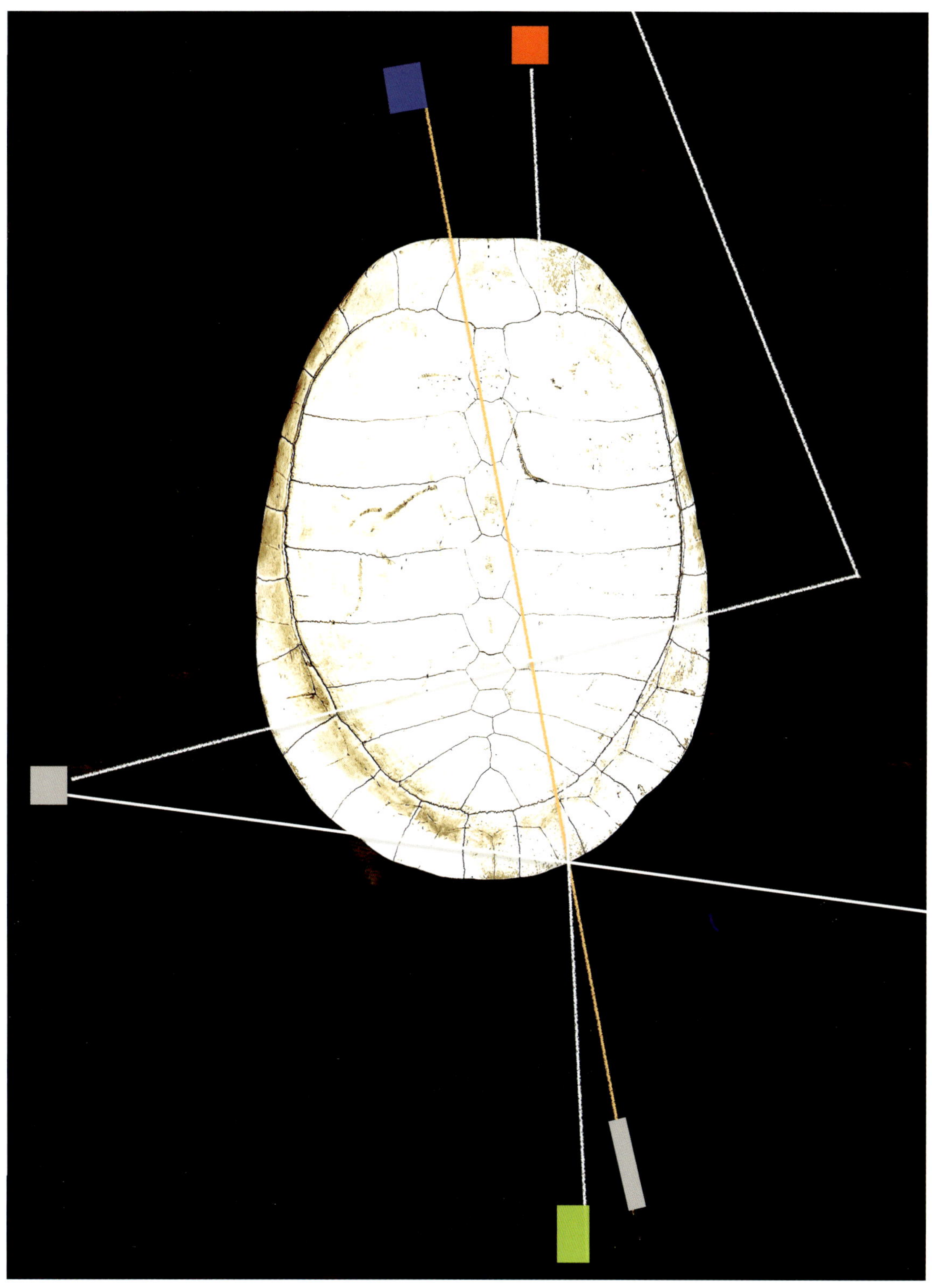

I should be hanging in the Louvre with Mondrian.

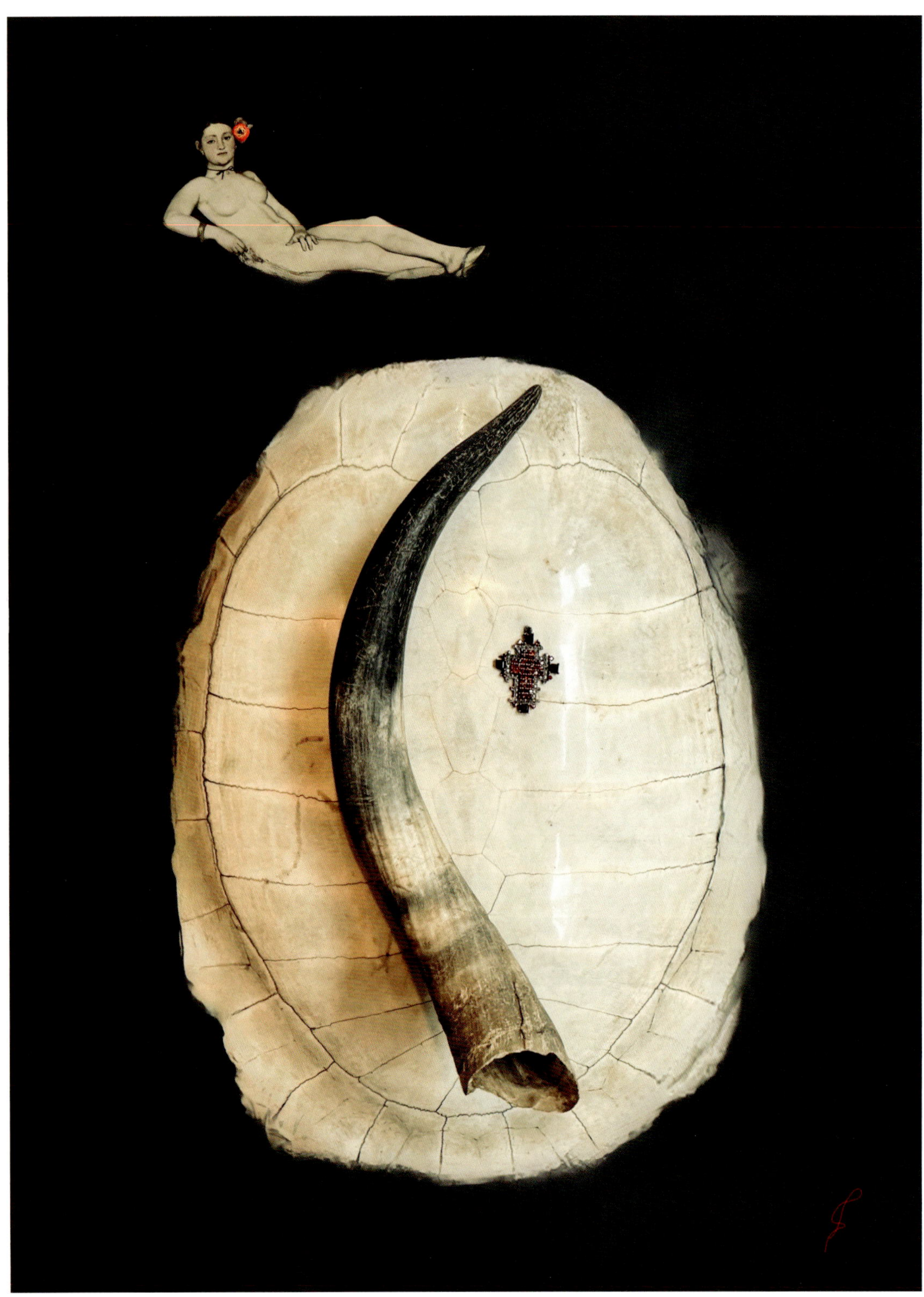

Mother Superior wouldn't approve, but who's going to tell?

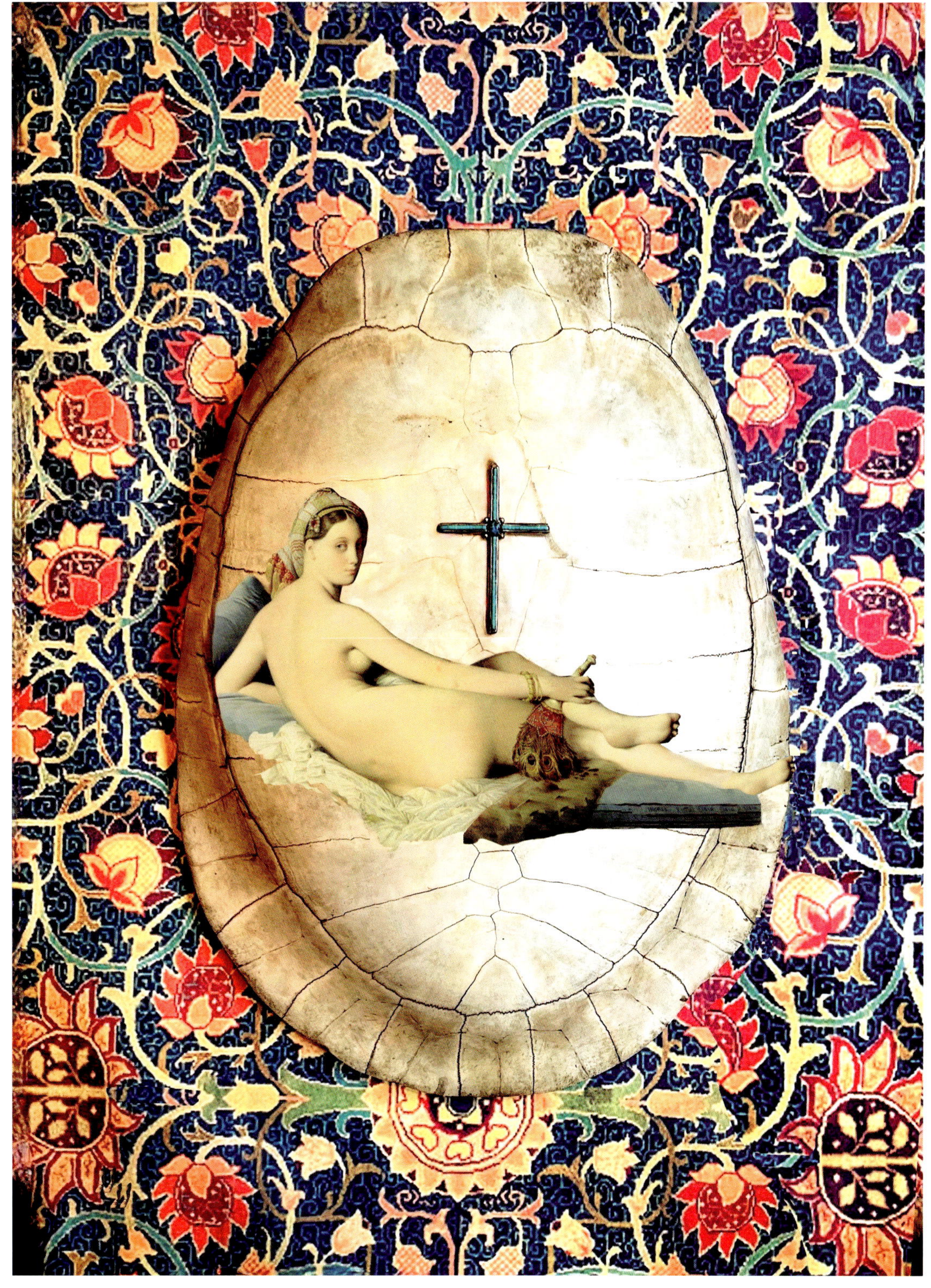

You're late.

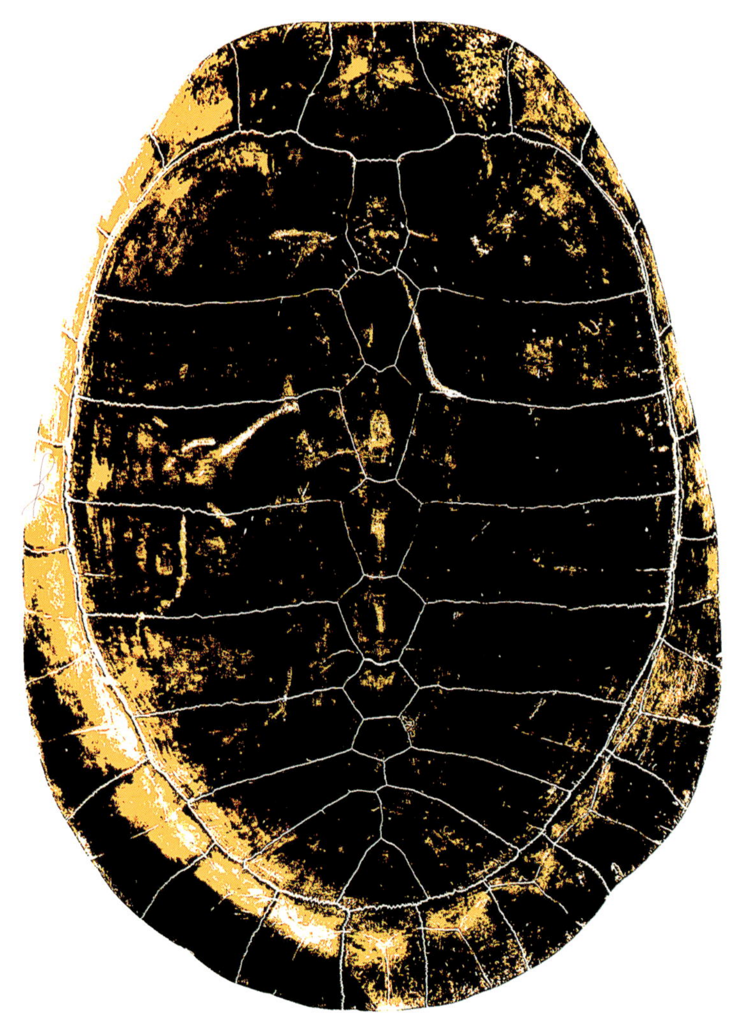

Darth Turtle.

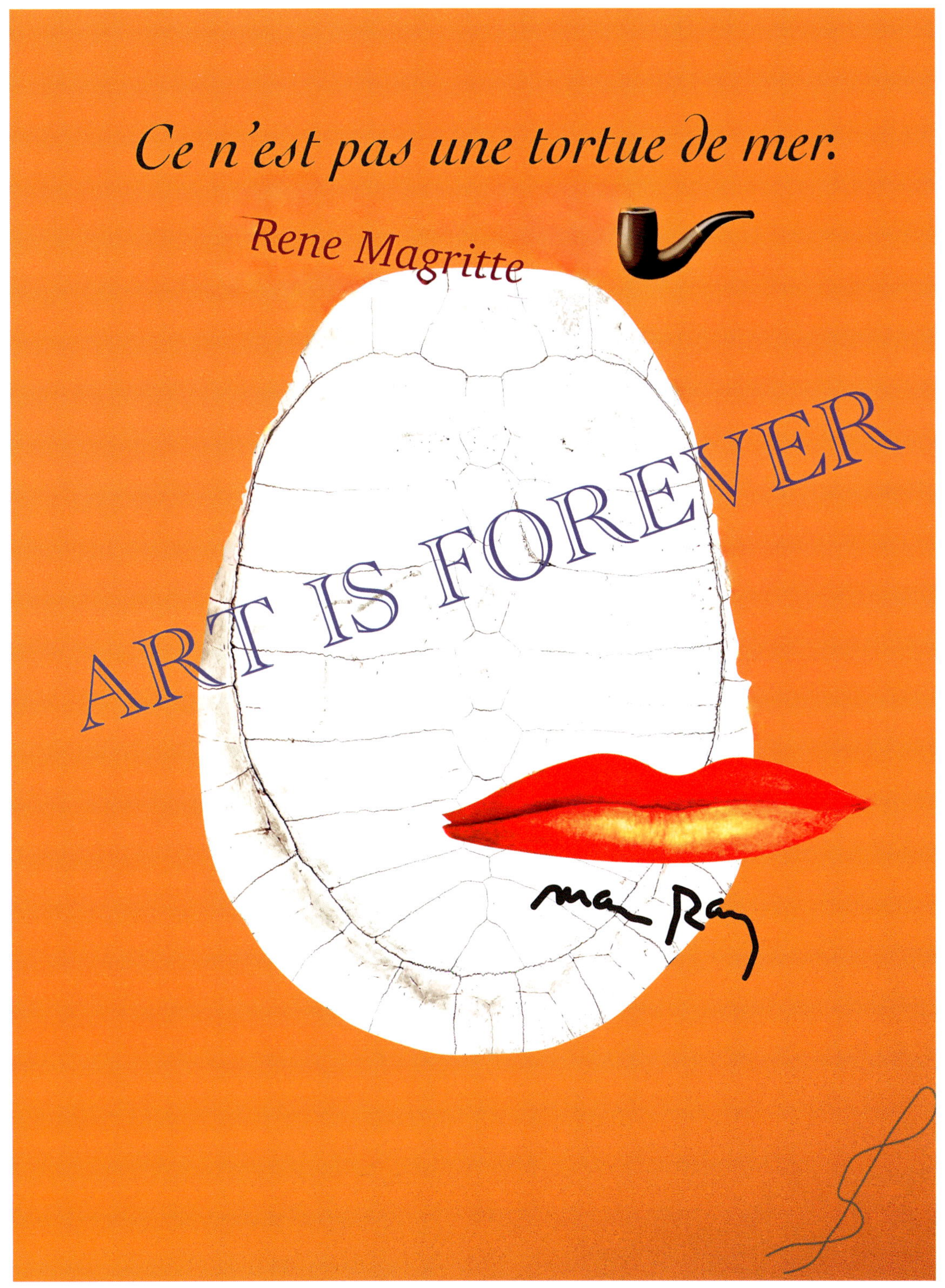

Sea Turtle Art School.

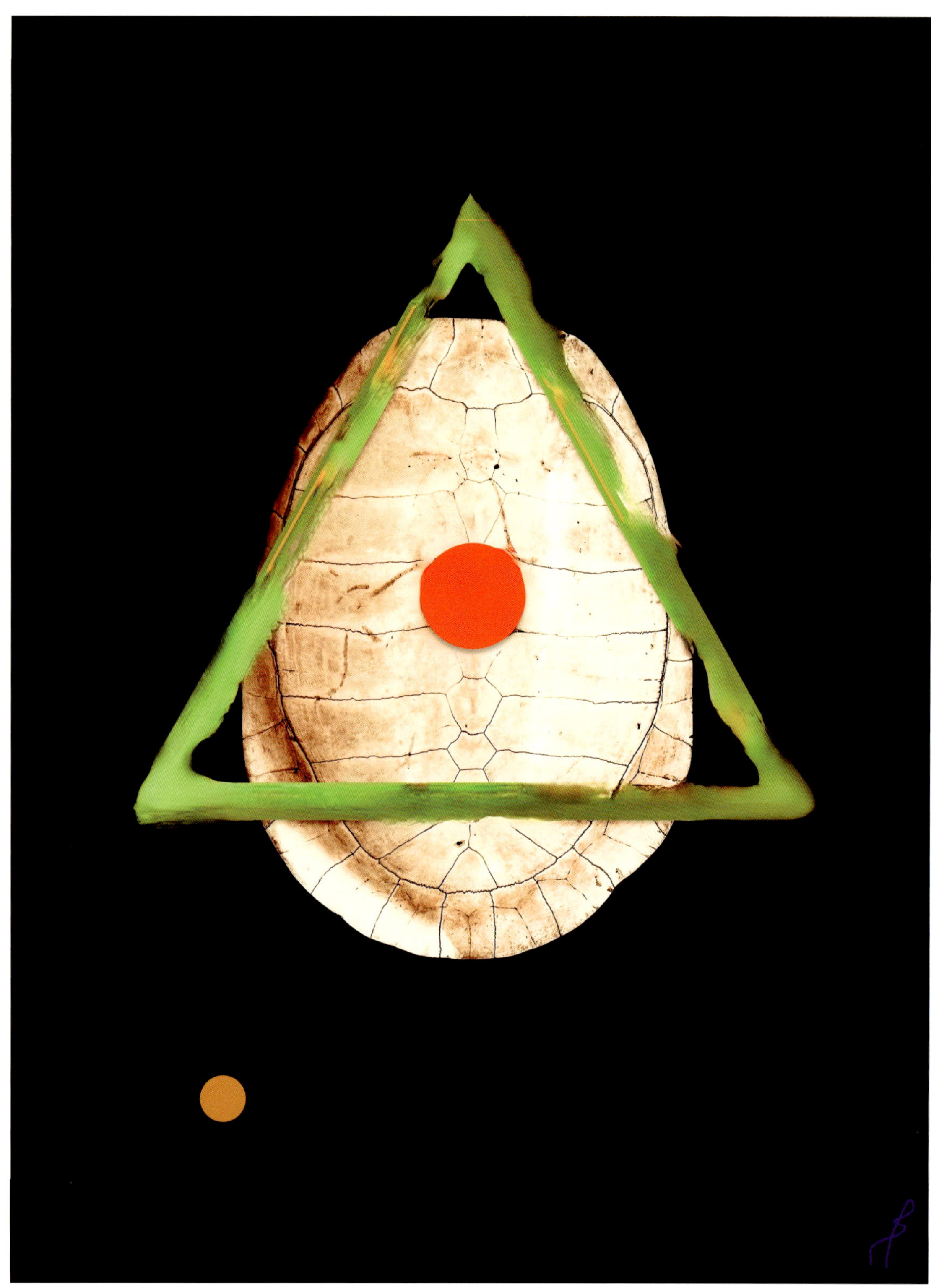

"I was never good at geometry."

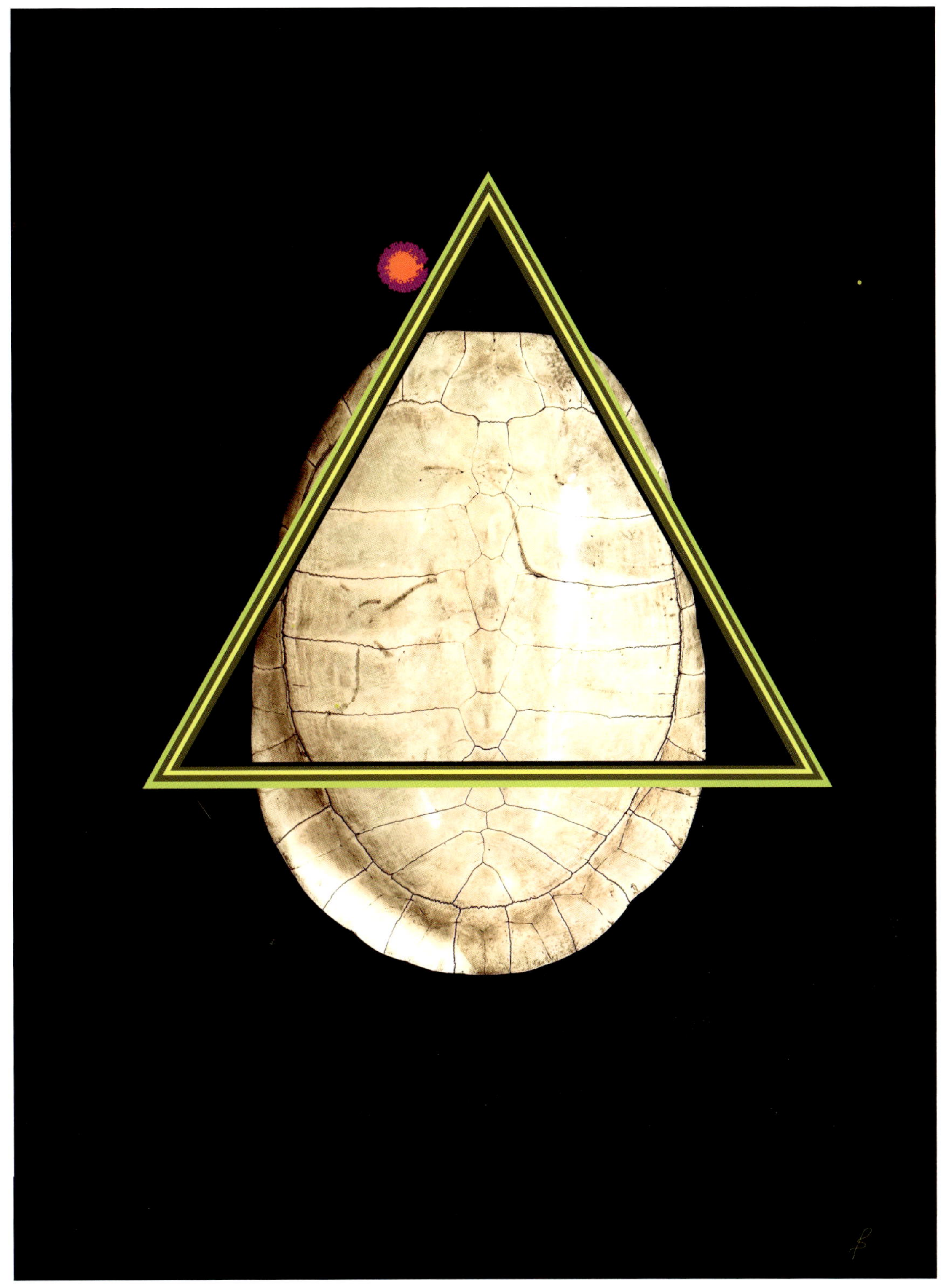

"I was good at everything."

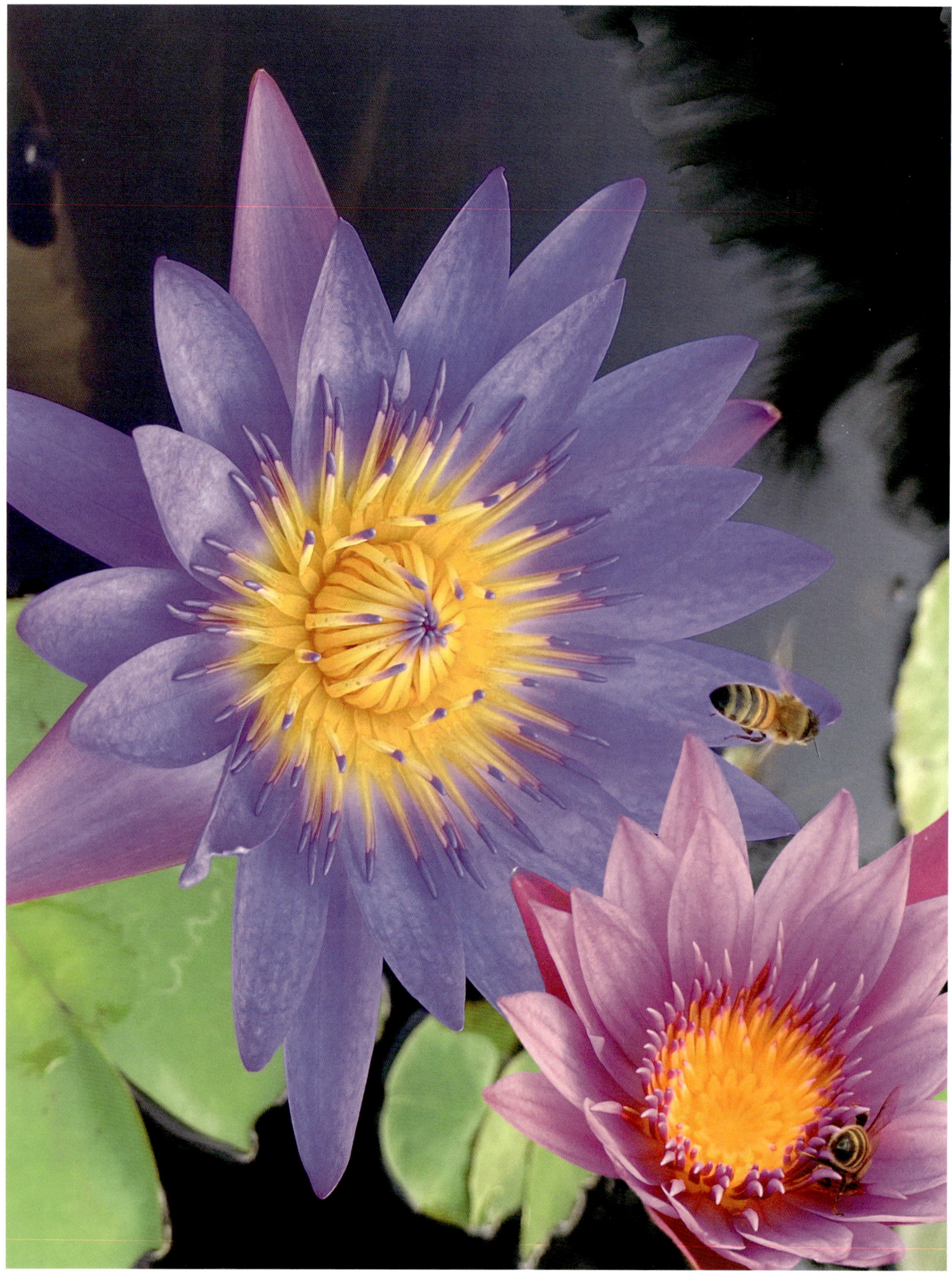

GATHERING FLOWERS

Look into a flower, and what do you see?

The very heart of nature's double nature? That is, the contending energies of creation and dissolution, the spiring toward complex form and the tidal pull away from it . . . the beauty of a flower and its rapid passing.

There, the achievement of order against all odds and its blithe abandonment. There, the perfection of art and the blind flux of nature. There, somehow, both transcendence and necessity.

Could that be right there in a flower the meaning of life?

Michael Pollan

In the beginning was Concept,

followed by creations of infinite varieties

even though time is an illusion.

PZS

Go to your fields and your gardens, and you shall learn
that it's the pleasure of the bee to gather honey of the flower,
But it is also the pleasure of the flower to yield its honey to the bee.
For to the bee a flower is a fountain of life,
And to the flower a bee is a messenger of love.

Kahlil Gibran

If I were a lily

I think I would wait all day

for the green face

of the hummingbird to touch me . . .

Mary Oliver

ODE TO A CALLA LILY

Swerve! Your leaf wraps round
your tiny flowers—male and female—
blooming in a spiral deep in your cup.

The spadix—a spike to be envied
by men and noted by women. . . .

How calmly you present yourself—

> not even a real lily
> toxic to dogs and cats
> once a symbol of death

> but that time is past
> though not for cats and dogs.

> Greedy, sway is not enough for you!
> Having no scent, you wear perfumed colors.

Is that what poison does?
Double down on enticement?

No matter.
We are seduced but will not eat you.

PZS

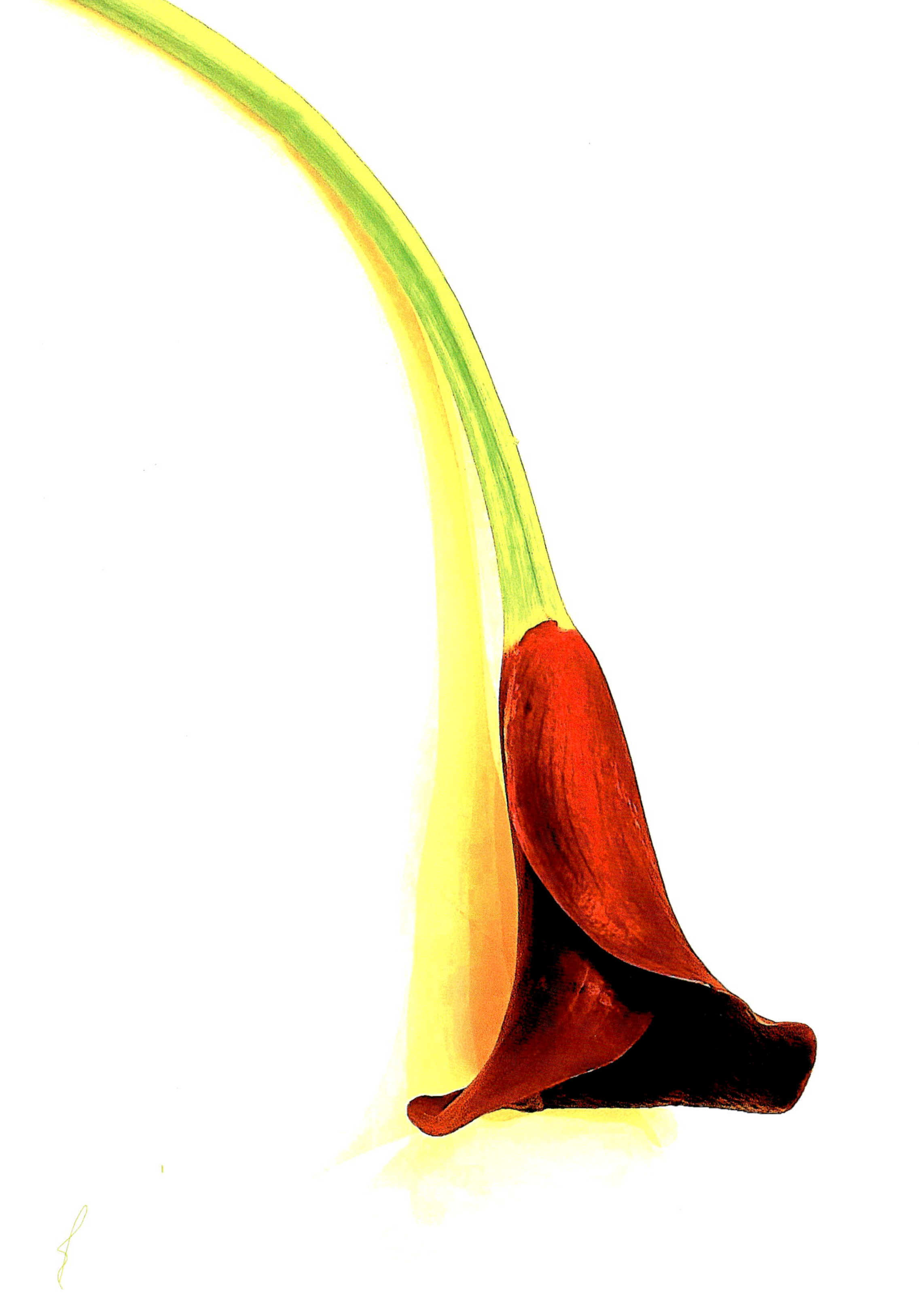

Hemerocallis fulva in its everyday clothes is a day lily, a tiger lily.

When she wears red, she is a fashion queen.

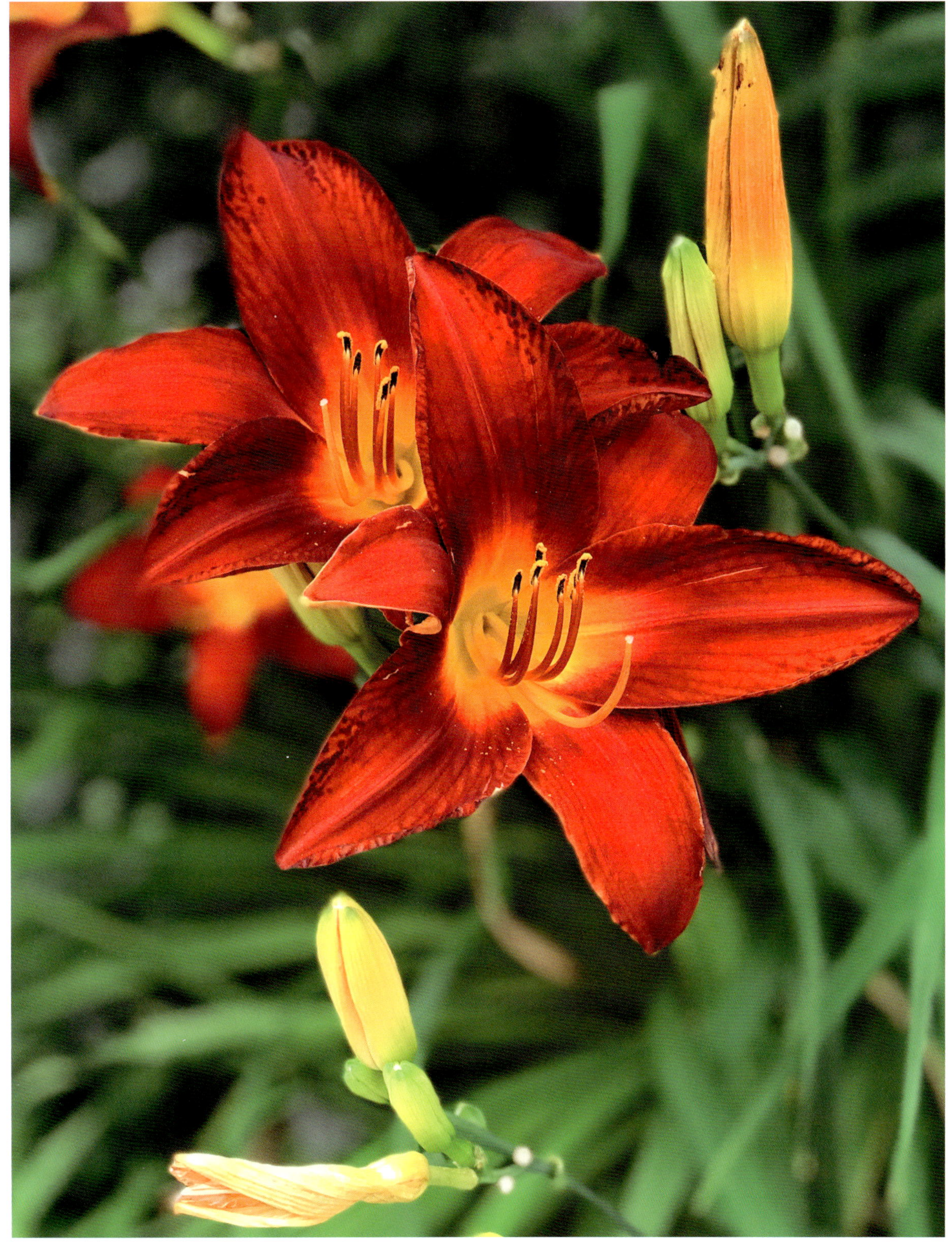

The Easter lily welcomes spring,

it tells me the long cold winter was a fling.

Paula Goldsmith

Lilium longiflorum

Easter lily
Trumpet lily

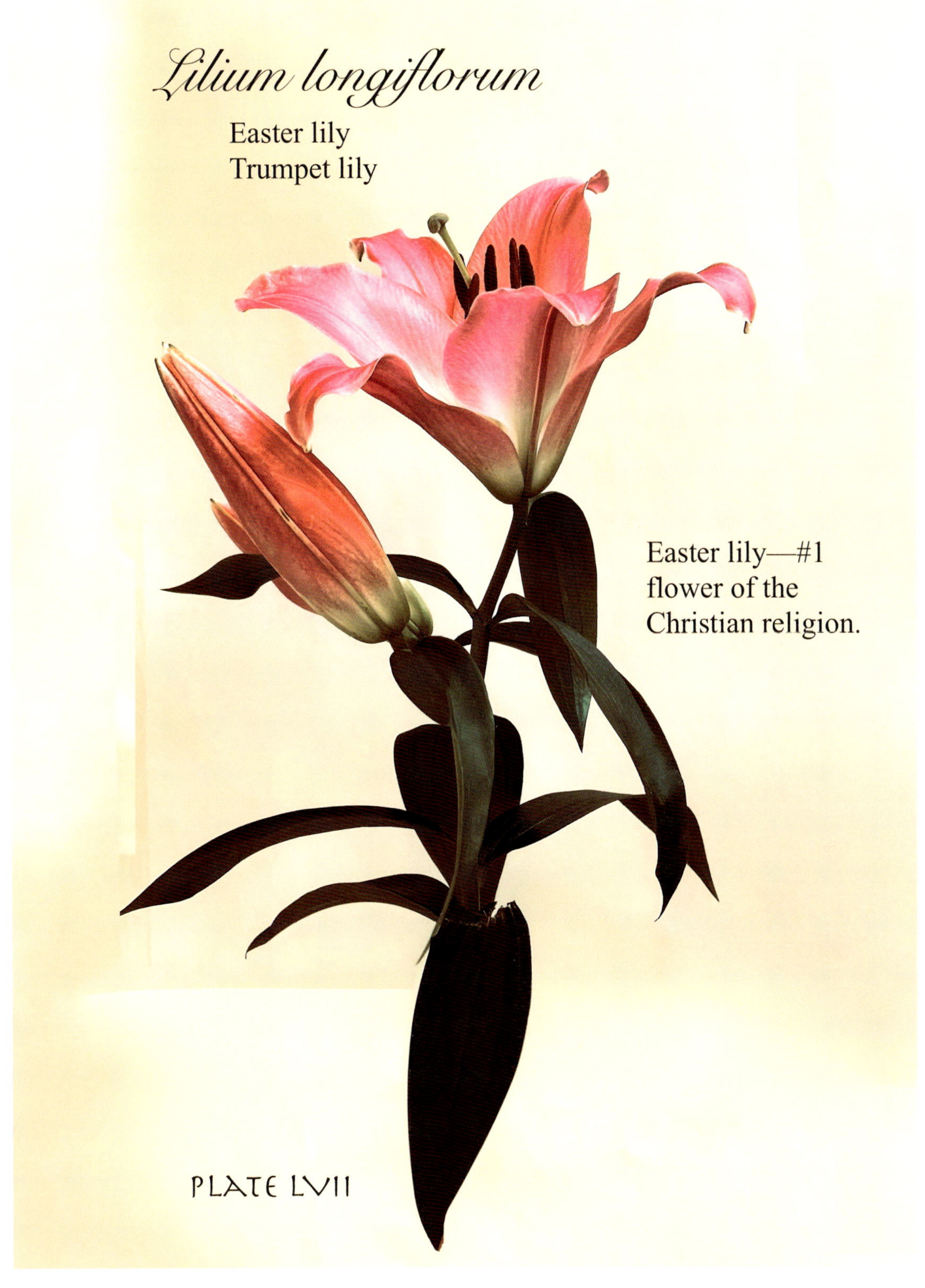

Easter lily—#1
flower of the
Christian religion.

PLATE LVII

The Sun is our gallant defender;
We thrive in his furious glow
Then withers the maize
In the blaze
Of his rays,
But we only flourish and grow.

Harry Edward Mills

Ah Sunflower! weary of time,
Who countest the steps of the Sun:
Seeking after that sweet golden clime
Where the traveler's journey is done.

Where the Youth pined away with desire,
And the pale Virgin shrouded in snow:
Arise from their graves and aspire,
Where my Sunflower wishes to go.

William Blake

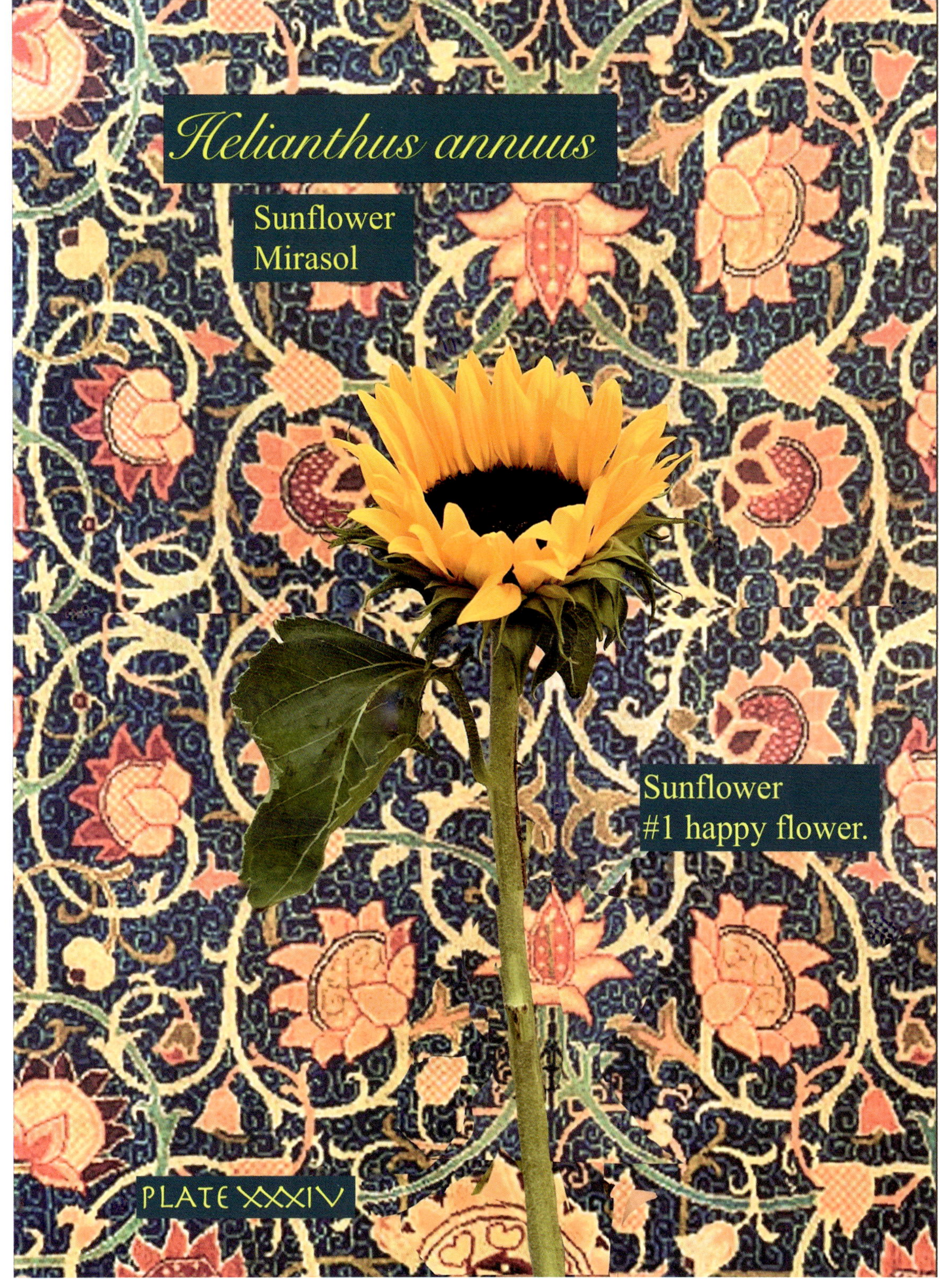

Helianthus annuus
Sunflower
Mirasol
Sunflower
#1 happy flower.
PLATE XXXIV

Anemone

give us wisdom

decreed

between your

open legs

a gateway to pathways

forgotten

vengeance

but never

shall we

repent

Ananda Belford

"Would you tell me, please, which way I ought to go from here?"

"That depends a good deal on where you want to get to," said the Cat.

"I don't much care where—" said Alice.

"Then it doesn't matter which way you go," said the Cat.

"—so long as I get somewhere," Alice added as an explanation.

"Oh, you're sure to do that," said the Cat, "if you only walk long enough."

Lewis Carroll

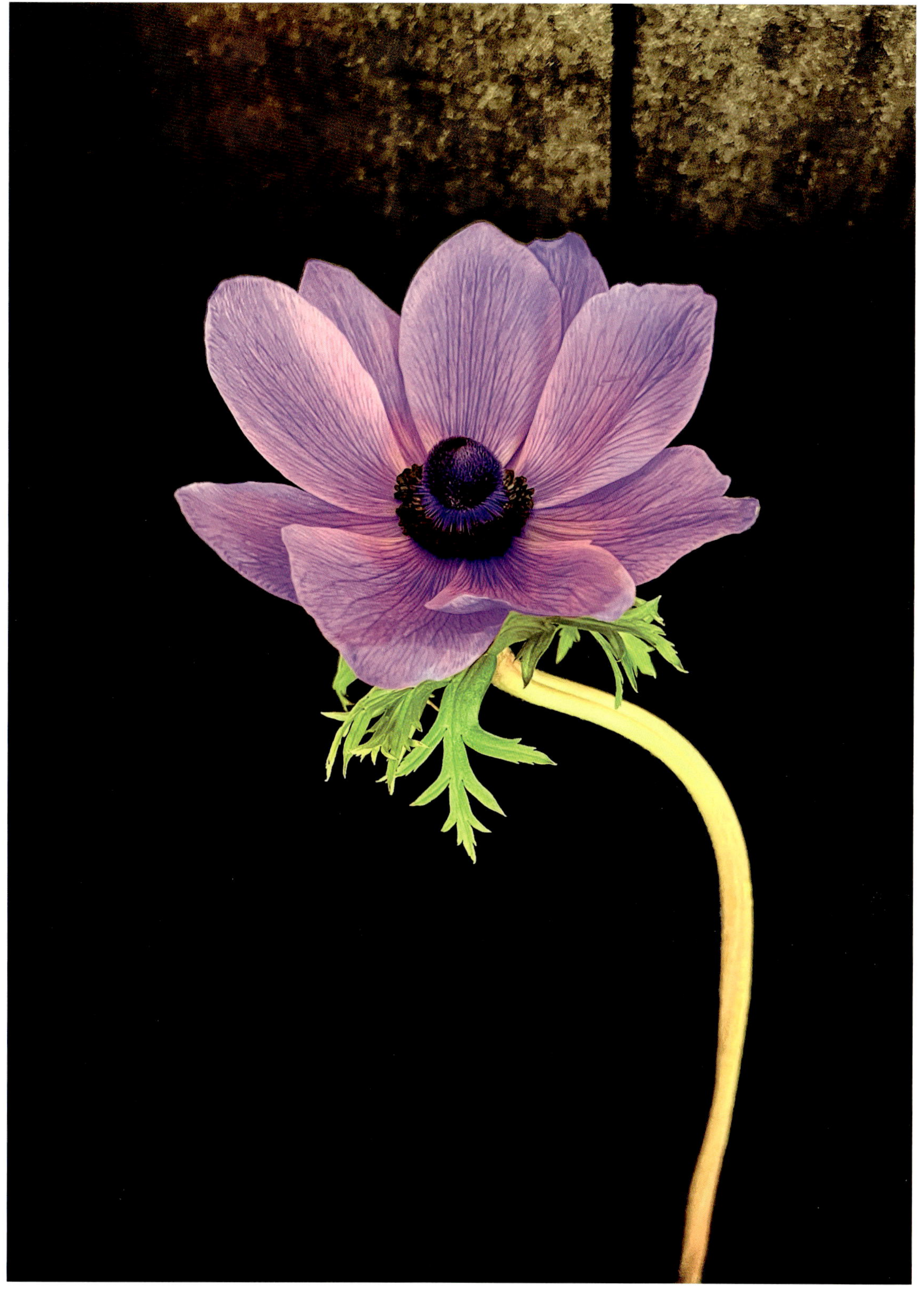

A rose is a rose is rose is a rose.

Gertrude Stein

The red rose whispers of passion,

And the white rose breathes of love;

Oh, the red rose is the falcon,

And the white rose is a dove.

But I send you a cream-white rose bud

With a flush on its petal tips;

For the love that is purest and sweetest

Has a kiss of desire on the lips.

John Boyle O'Reilly

It is not our job to identify the secret of the red rose

Maybe our job is to dive into the magic of the red rose

And camp behind the wisdom

Wash our hand in the glory of a green leaf and go our way.

Sohrab Sepehri

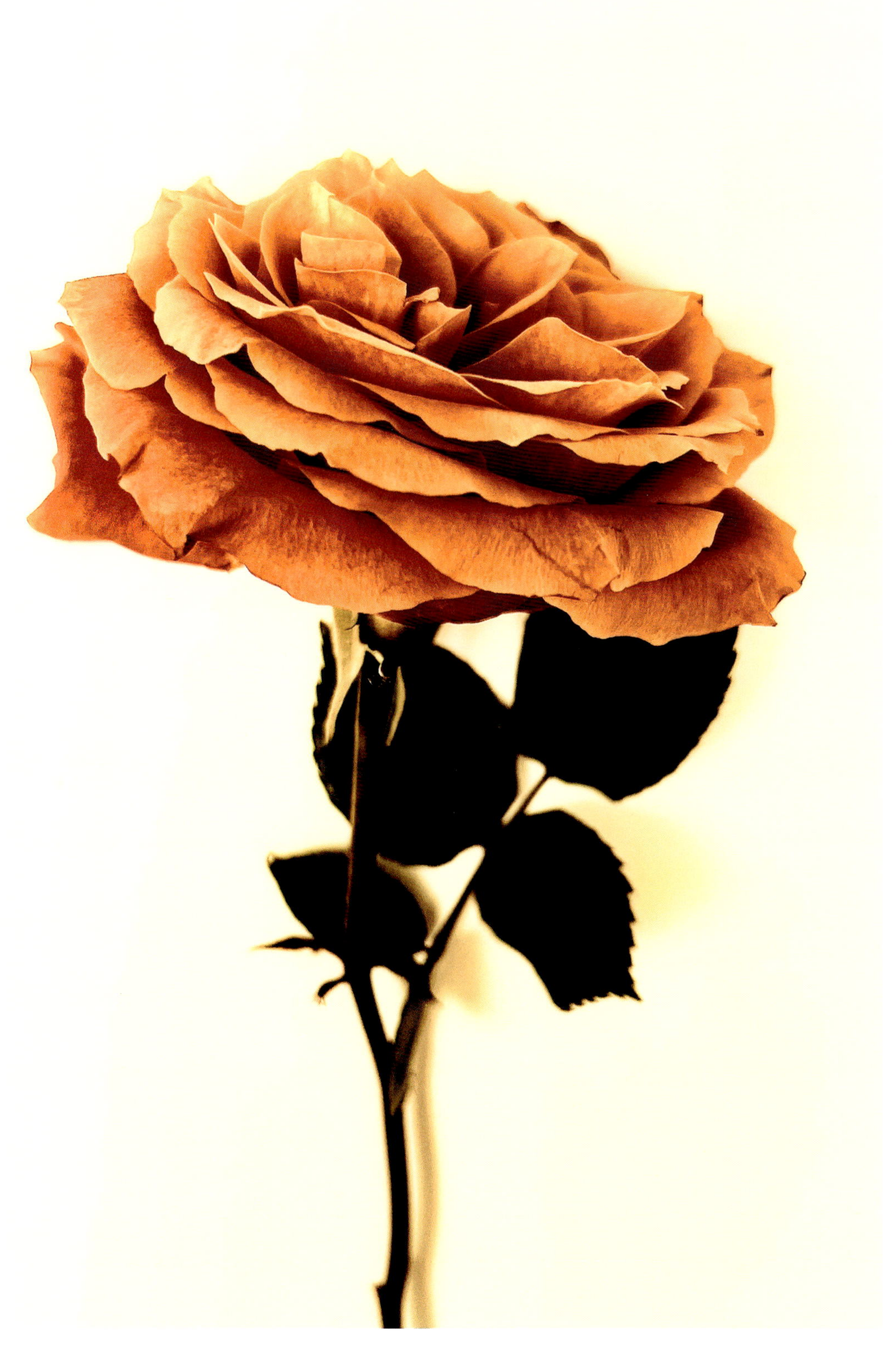

A flash of dew, a bee or two,

A breeze

A caper in the trees —

And I'm a rose.

Emily Dickinson

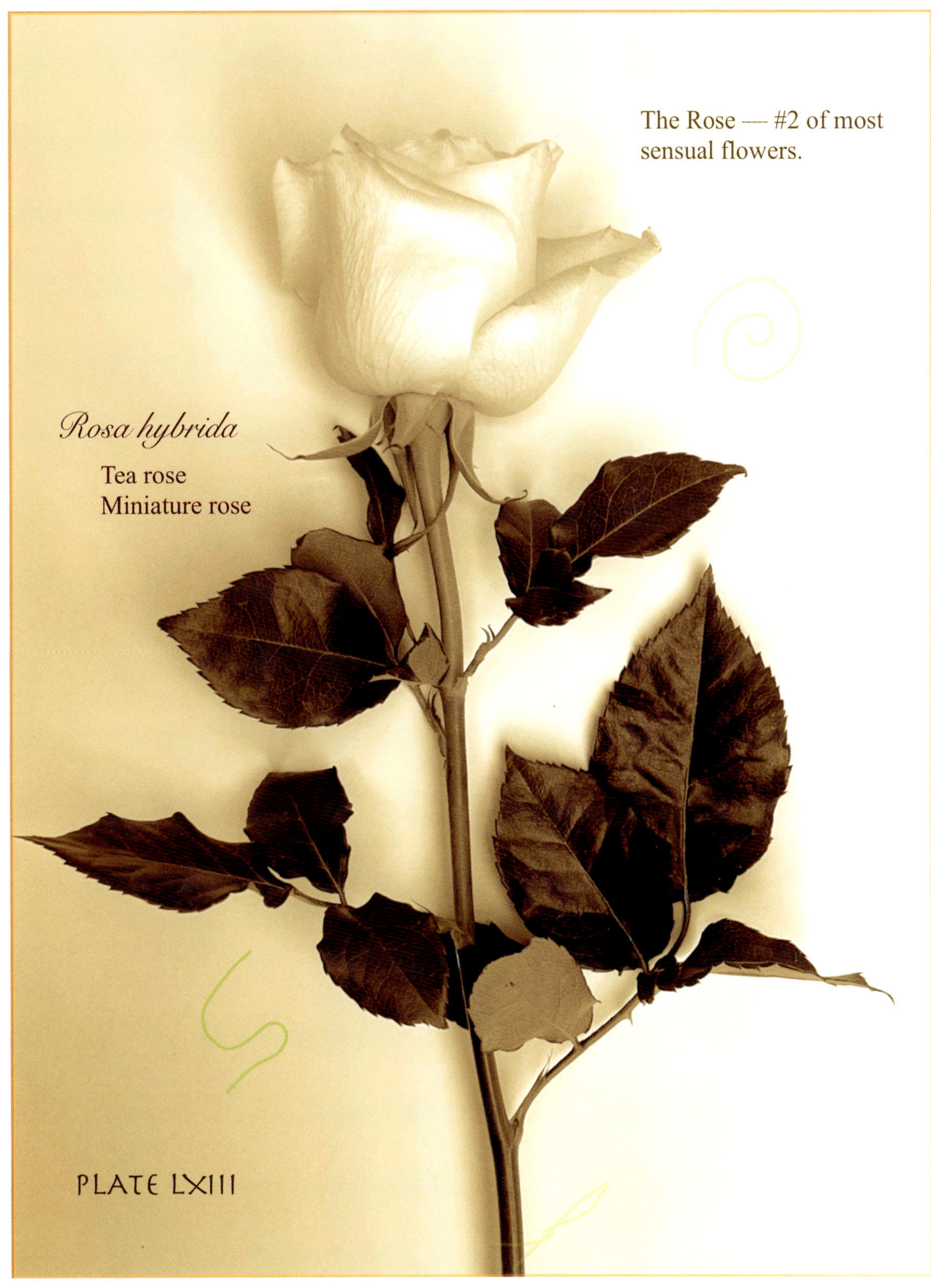

The Rose — #2 of most sensual flowers.

Rosa hybrida
Tea rose
Miniature rose

PLATE LXIII

Roses are beautiful for a show

Daisies are nicer for their peaceful nature

But if it's true love you want to show

A red tulip is the way to go. . .

Belinda Hicks

If only people were more like tulips and could somehow find a way

To grace this world with beauty before they slowly fade away.

Jim Yerman

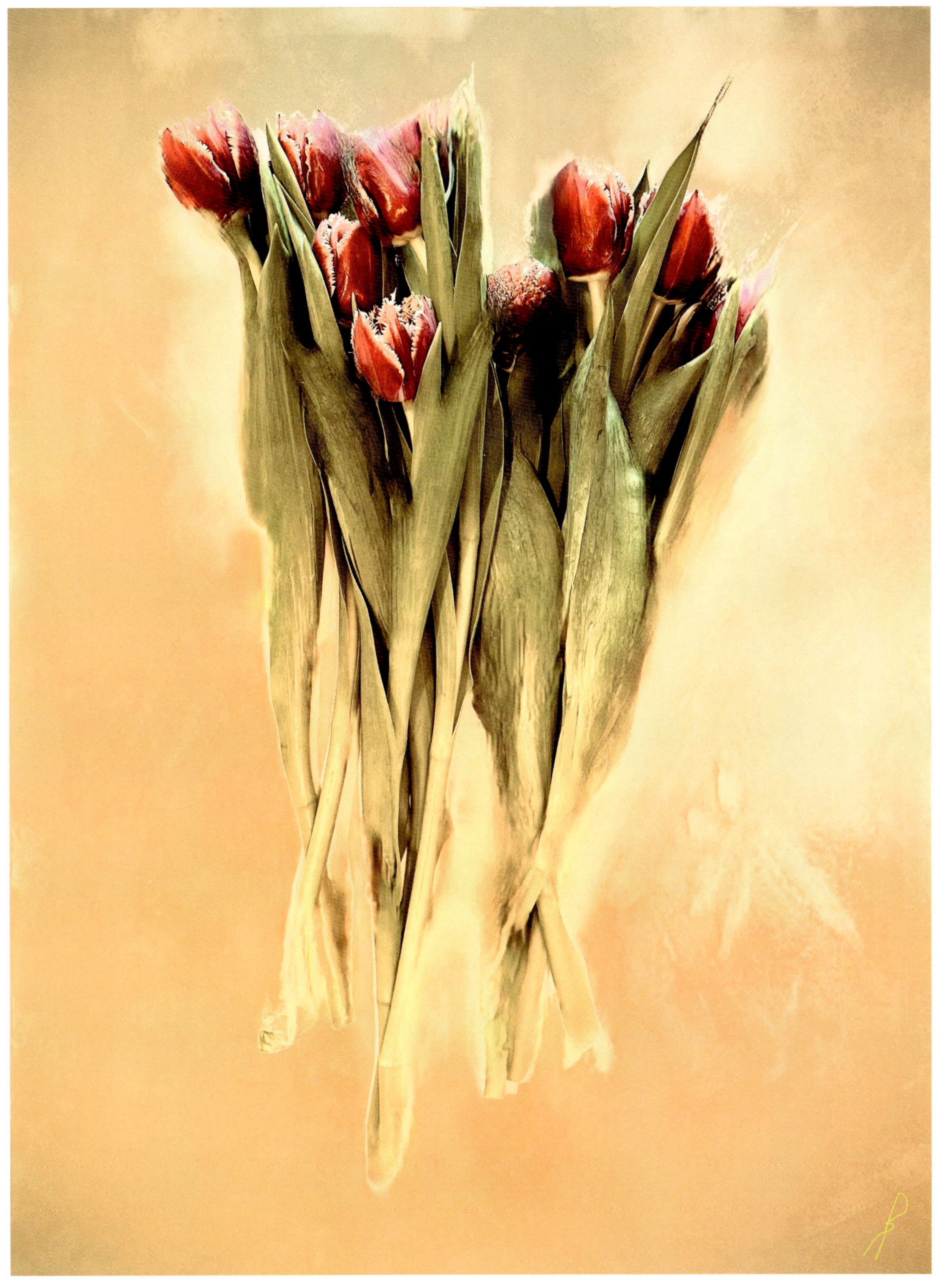

What words can describe this Amaryllis divine?

Certainly not any of mine.

Look at how red!

As though the Universe had bled.

Etienne Charilaou

I am so spectacular I simply put others to shame.
From a large bulb my green shoots will grow. I dwarf
the other plants. I love to be on show . . . My trumpets
are enormous, people stand and gaze at them.

I have no scent for you to smell when I am flowering.
The intensity of my blooms would make it overpowering.

Jan Allison

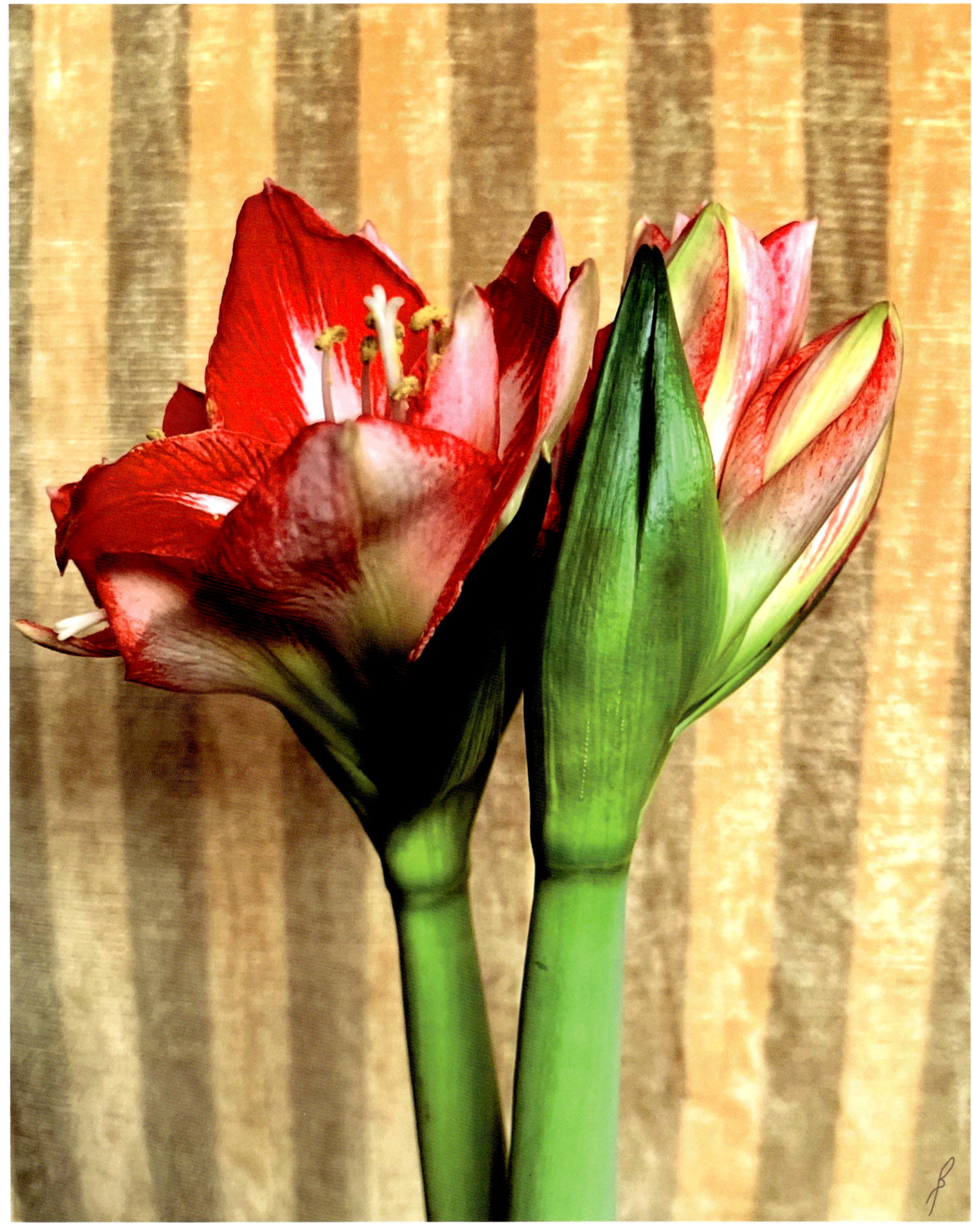

Just as I wonder whether it's going to die,

the orchid blossoms and I can't explain why it

moves my heart, why such pleasure

comes from one small bud on a long spindly stem, one

blood red gold flower opening at mid-summer,

tiny, perfect in its hour.

Sam Hamil

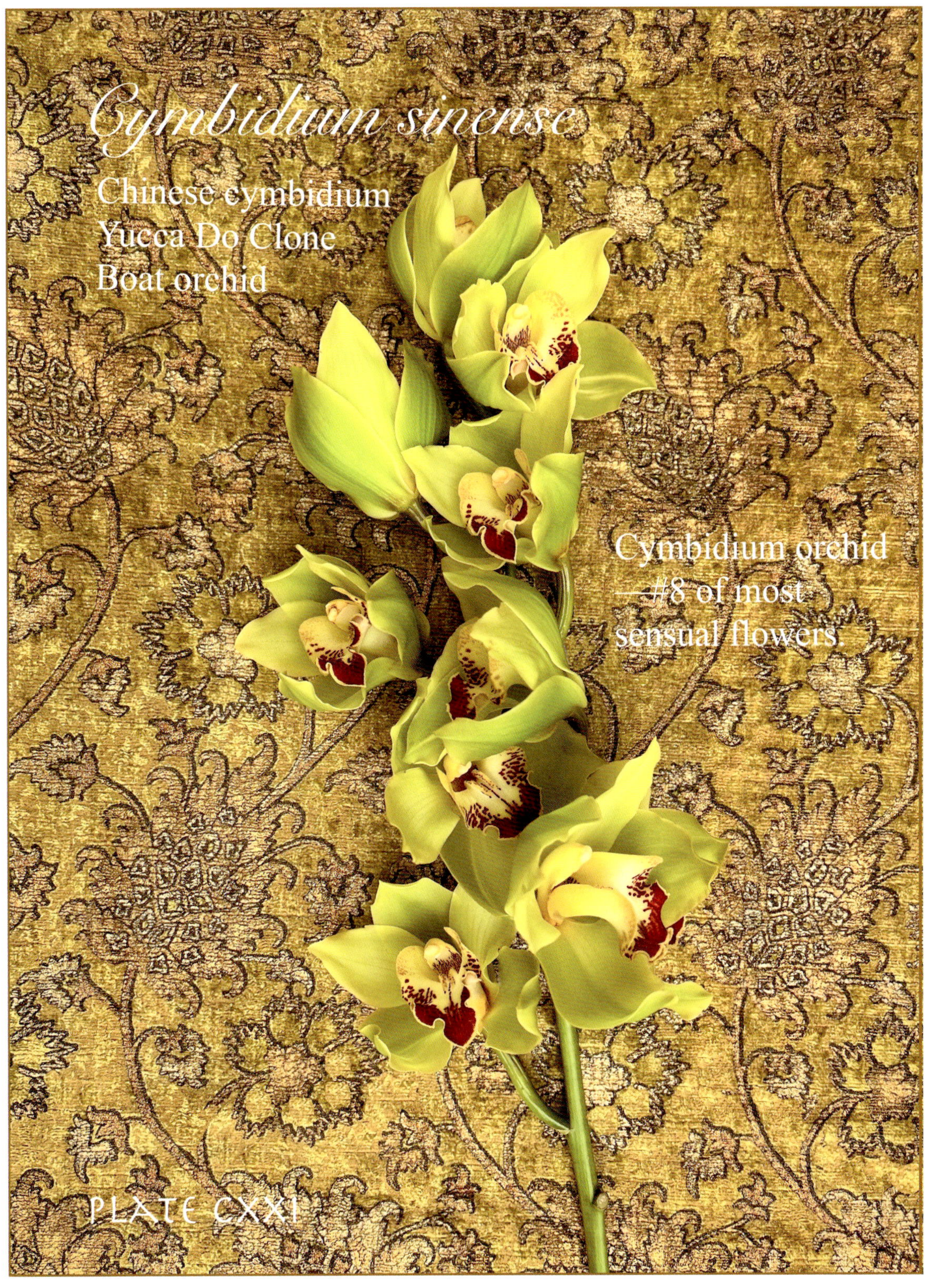

Cymbidium sinense
Chinese cymbidium
Yucca Do Clone
Boat orchid
Cymbidium orchid
—#8 of most
sensual flowers.
PLATE CXXI

I've caught myself talking to my orchid.

Surprise myself when I call her, Baby,

As in: Baby, you could use some water. . .

She never utters a word,

But, man,

Does she bloom with purity!

Francie Lynch

ORCHID SCREEN

Come not at dawn,
For I am weary when the morning breaks
After a long night spent in dreams of you.

Come not at noon.
When footsteps clatter round the splashing well
And shrill tones jangle by the gatehouse door.

But come at night
When flowers of moonlight in the courtyard bloom
And moonlight shadows paint the orchid screen,
One shadow yours—another shadow mine.

ancient Korean poem,
translated by Joan Grigsby

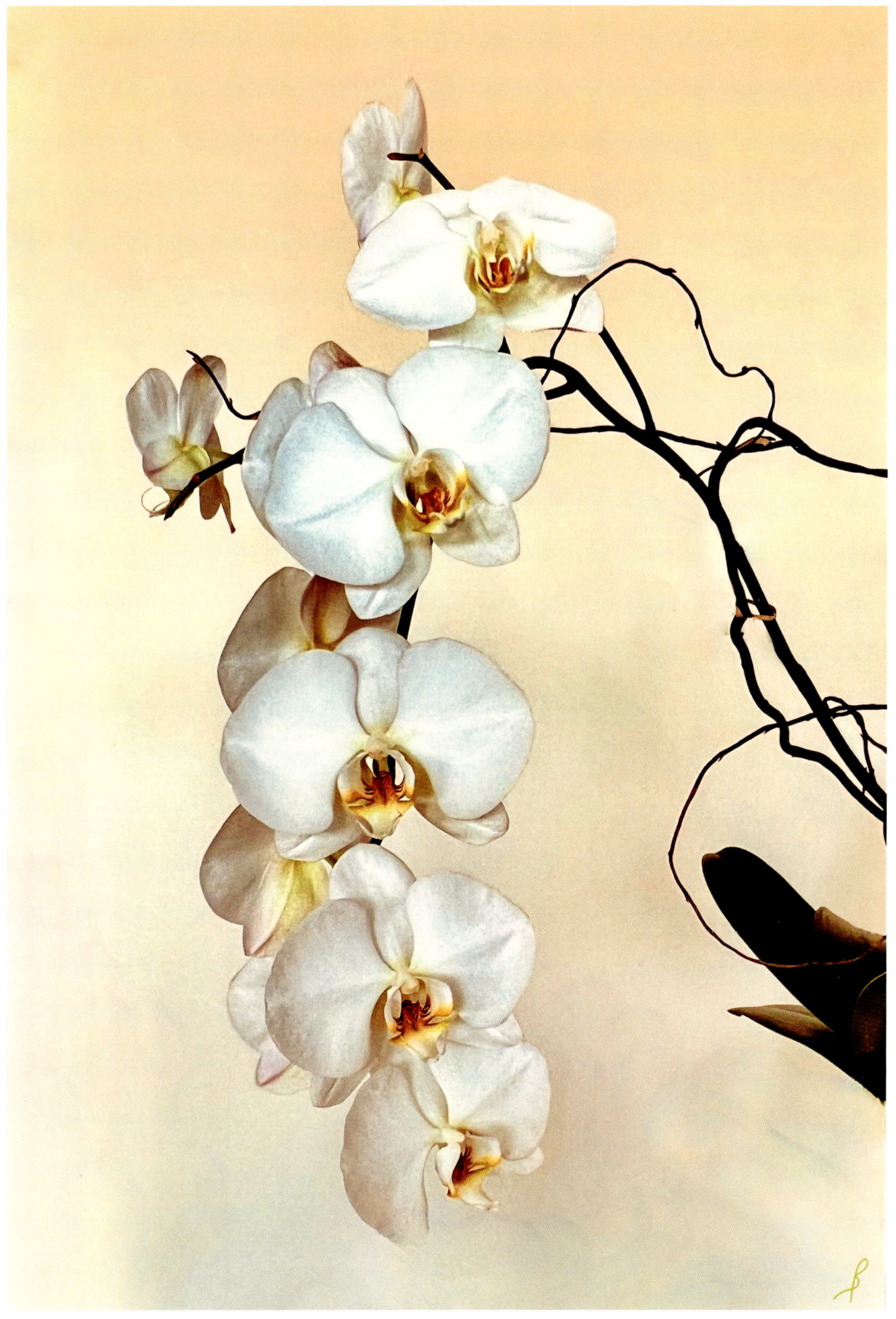

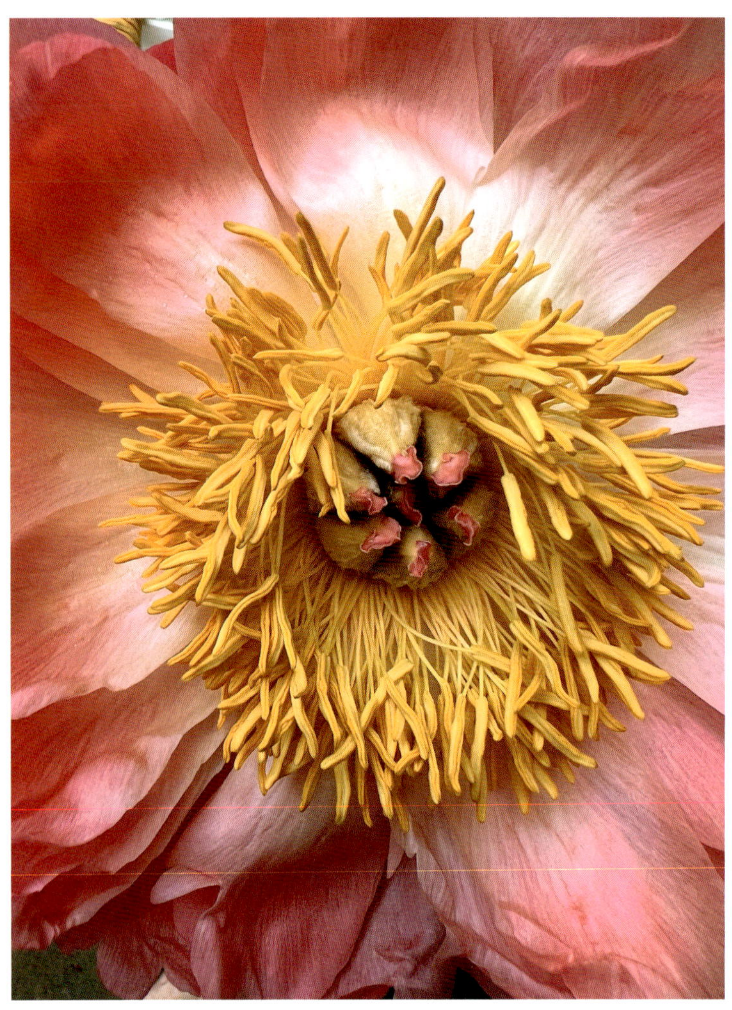

This morning the green fists of the peonies are getting ready
to break my heart
as the sun rises,
as the sun strokes them with his old, buttery fingers

and they open ---
pools of lace,
white and pink ---
and all day the black ants climb over them.

Mary Oliver

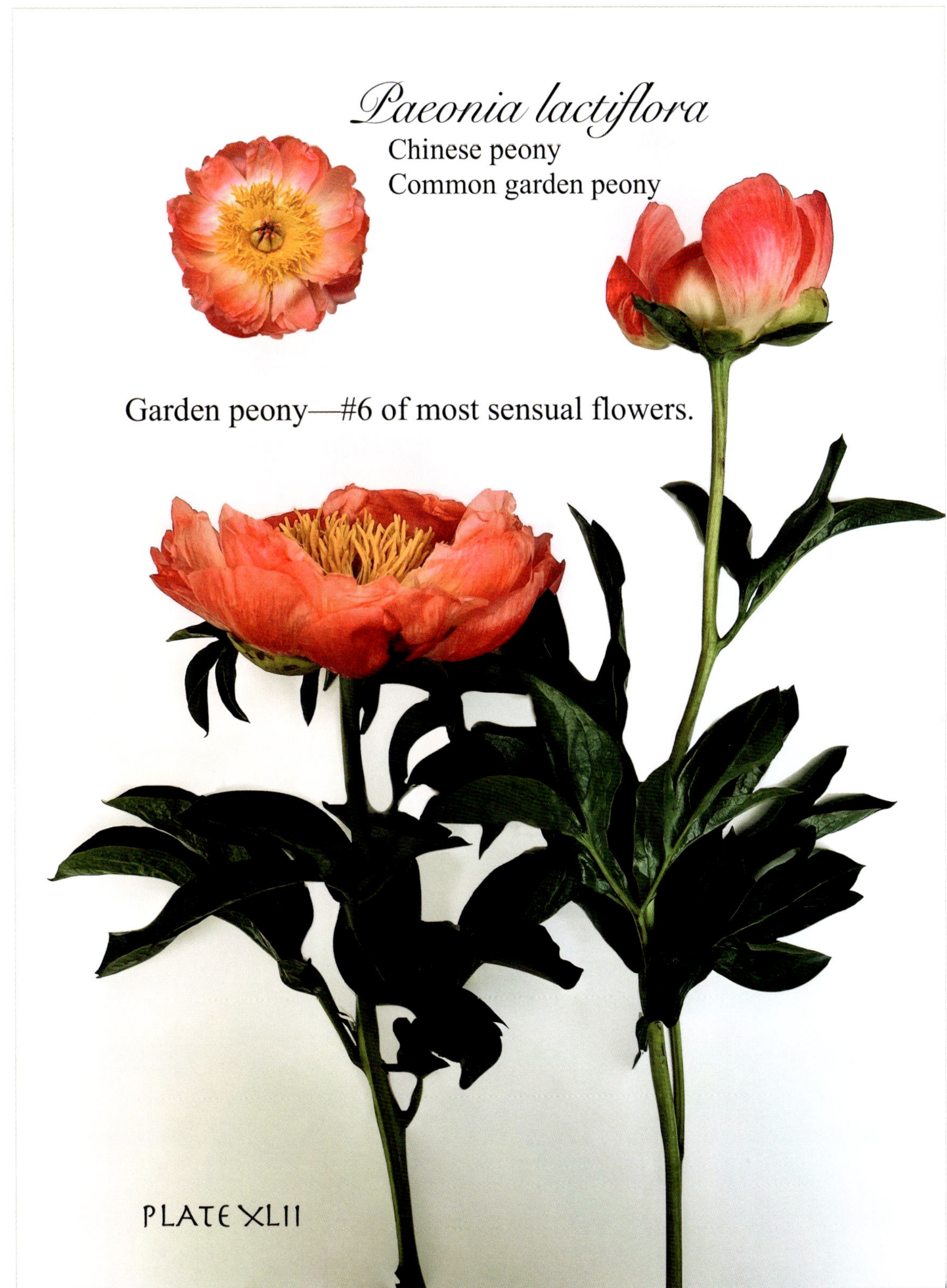

Paeonia lactiflora
Chinese peony
Common garden peony
Garden peony—#6 of most sensual flowers.
PLATE XLII

No one celebrates the allium.

The way each purposeful stem

ends in a globe, a domed umbel,

makes people think,

'Drumsticks,' and that's that.

Besides, it's related to the onion.

Is that any reason for disregard?

The flowers - look -

are bouquets of miniature florets. . .

Denise Levertov

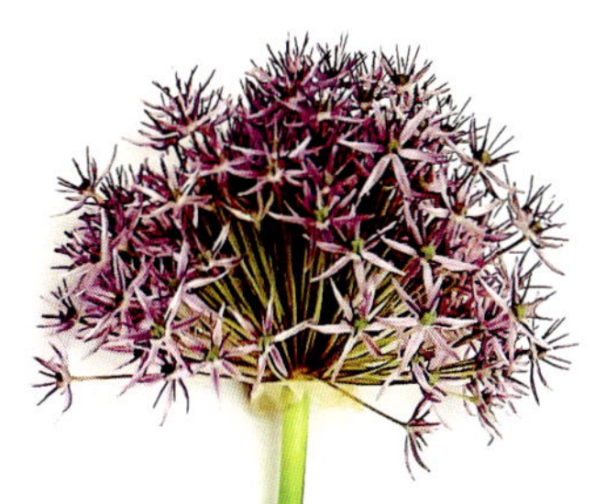

Giant Allium — #27 of
most sensual flowers.

#5 of related to desired
food genus.

Allium giganteum

Giant allium
Ornamenal onion
Ornamental garlic

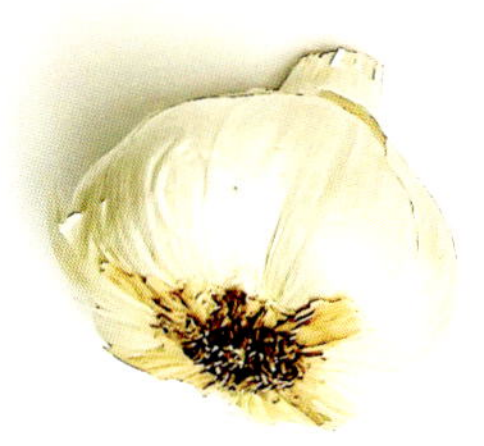

PLATE XIV

What would I have become;

If I were allowed to be as the Iris

Living my Life; Veridicality.*

Geraldine Baugh

*Veridicality: truthful, veracious, non-illusory

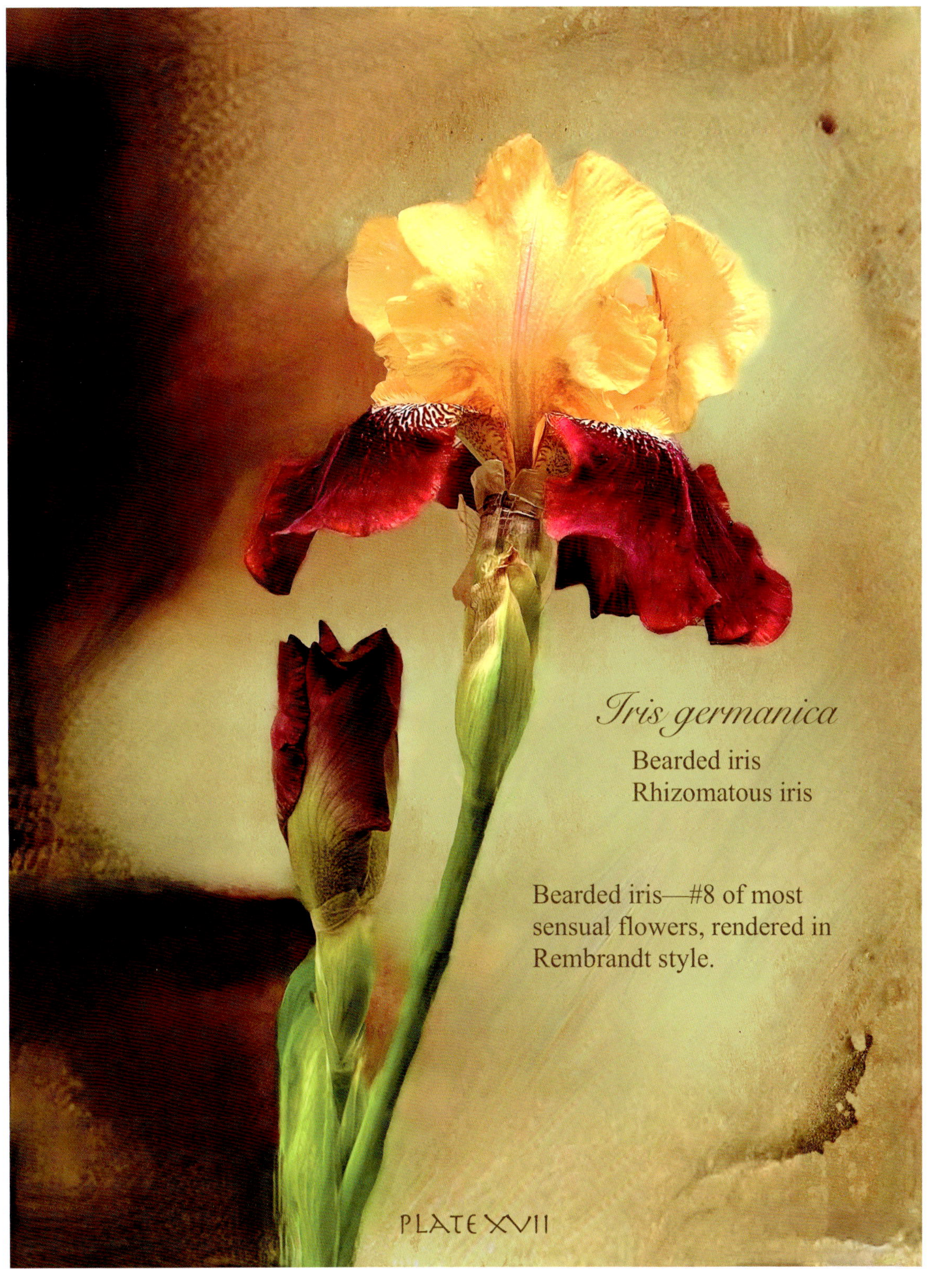

Iris germanica

Bearded iris
Rhizomatous iris

Bearded iris—#8 of most
sensual flowers, rendered in
Rembrandt style.

PLATE XVII

White Iris was a princess

In a kingdom long ago,

Mysterious as moonlight

And silent as the snow. . . .

How kind that earth should treasure

So beautiful a thing —

All mystical enchantment,

To stir our hearts in spring!

Bliss Carman

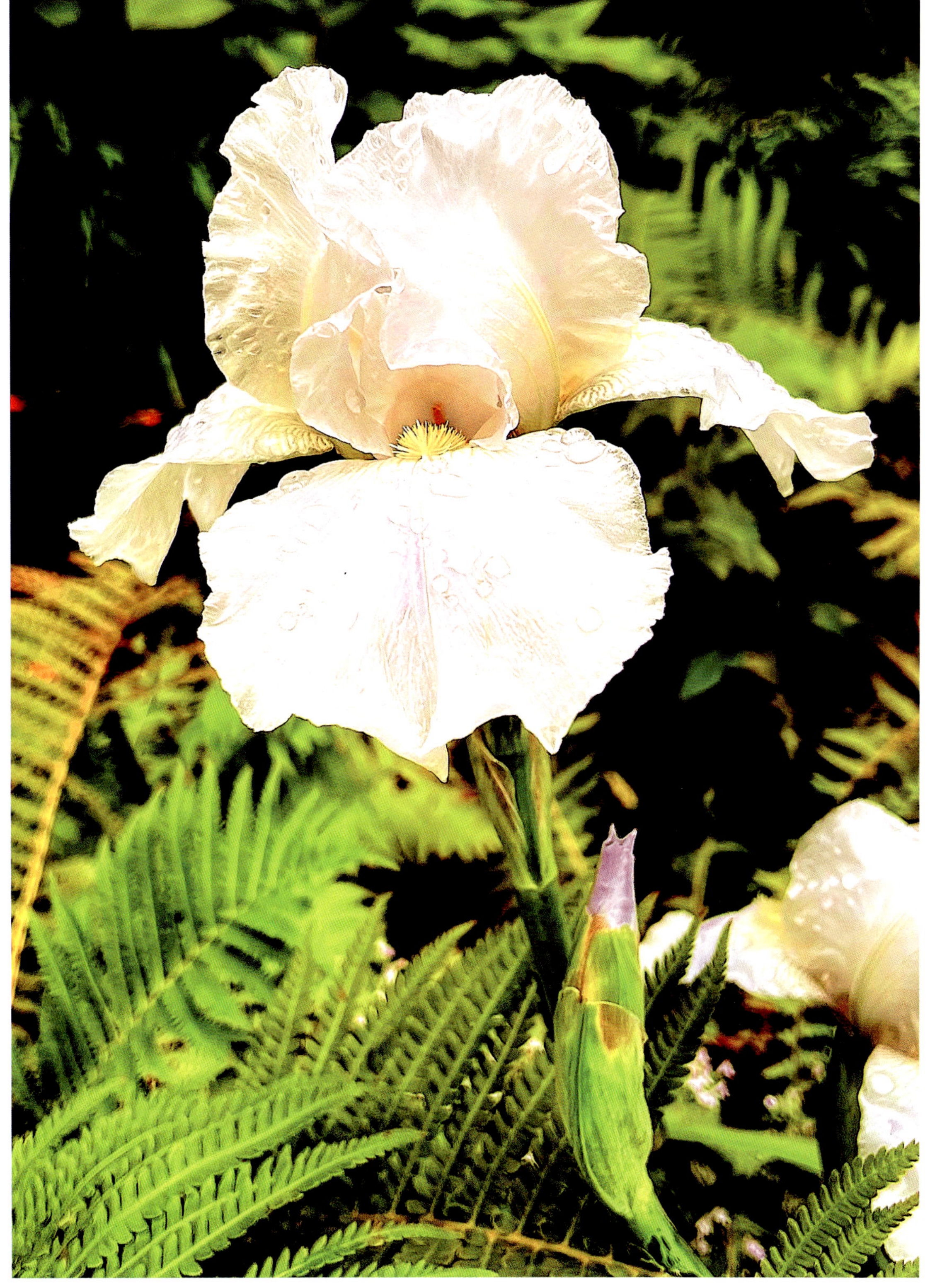

At the bottom of the ridge by stream banks

The light has gentled, monarch butterflies and hummingbird moths

Sip the sugared nectar lying languid in the milkweed blossoms. . .

And you, lying under the milkweed,

Enter into the stillness of night,

From where you are,

You can hear their dreams.

Dylan Thomas

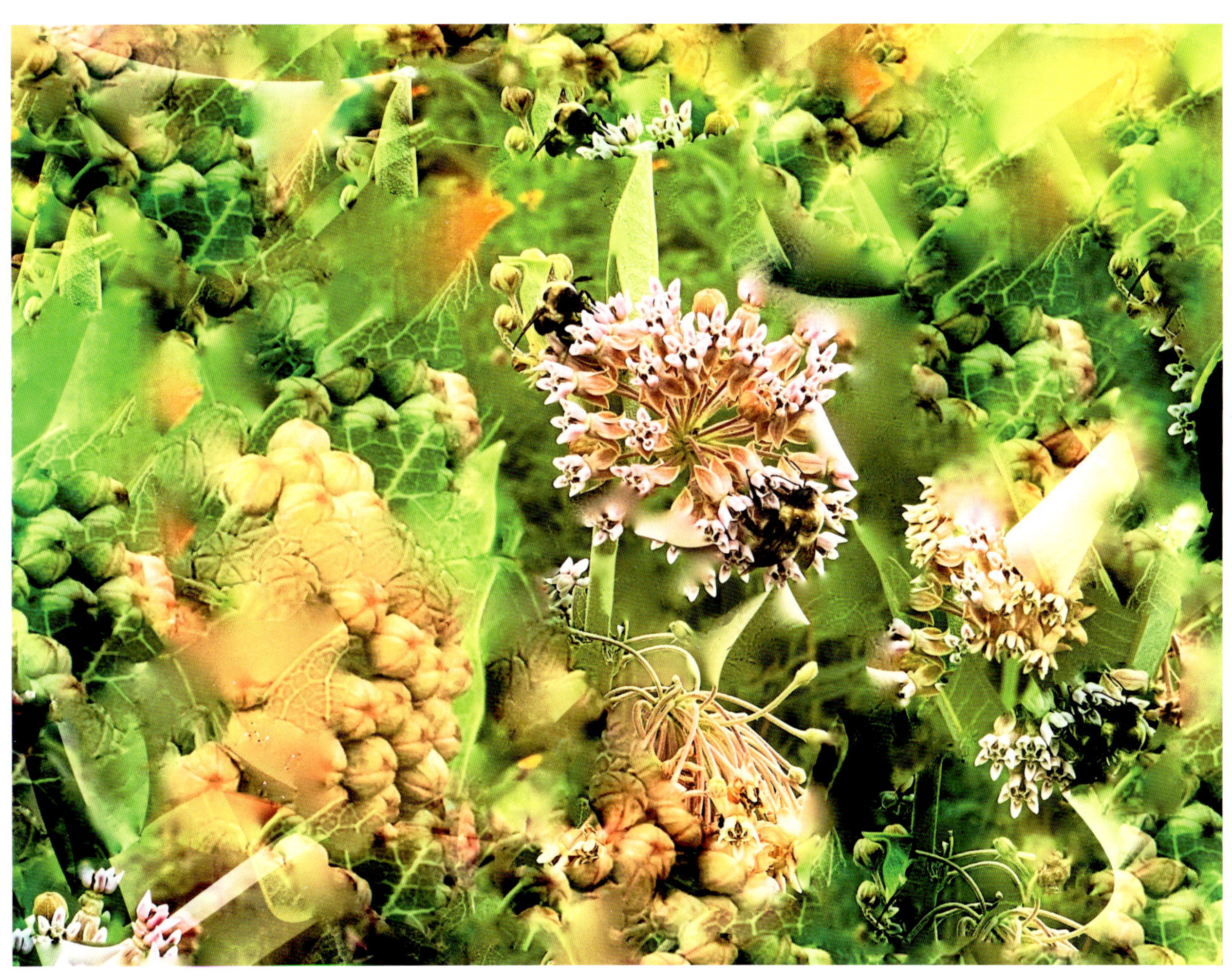

I tell myself softly, *this is how love begins—*

the air alive with something inconceivable,

seeds of every imaginable possibility

floating across the wet grasses, under

the thin arms of ferns. It drifts like snow

or old ash, settling on the dust of the roadways

as you and I descend into thickets, flanked

by the fragrance of honeysuckle and white

primrose.

Bradford Tice

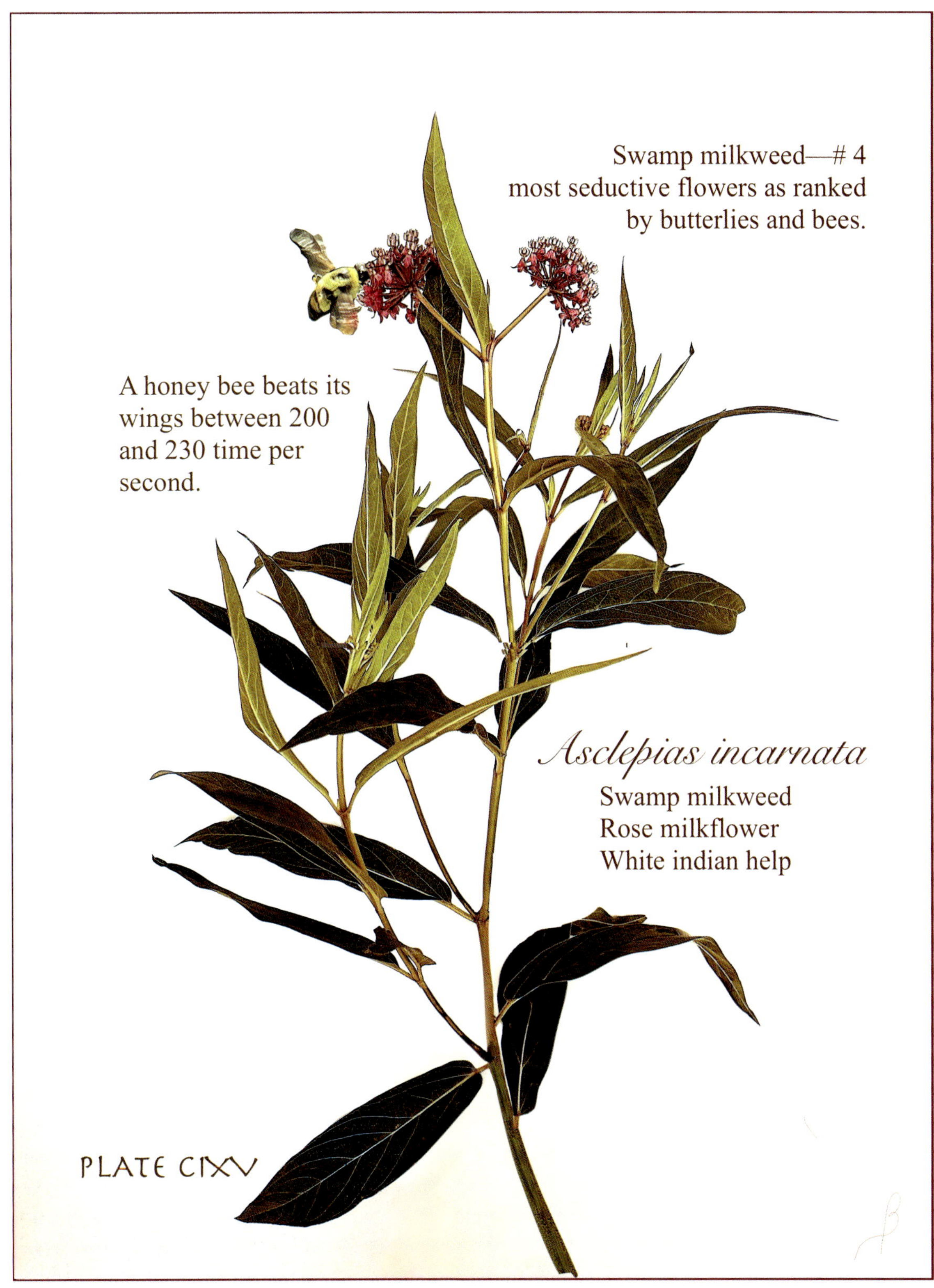

Swamp milkweed—# 4
most seductive flowers as ranked
by butterlies and bees.

A honey bee beats its
wings between 200
and 230 time per
second.

Asclepias incarnata
Swamp milkweed
Rose milkflower
White indian help

PLATE CIXV

You grow on my soul like a hidden plant.

And whenever you are going to bloom

My heart is going to explode like the blossom of hydrangea in May.

Nefelibata

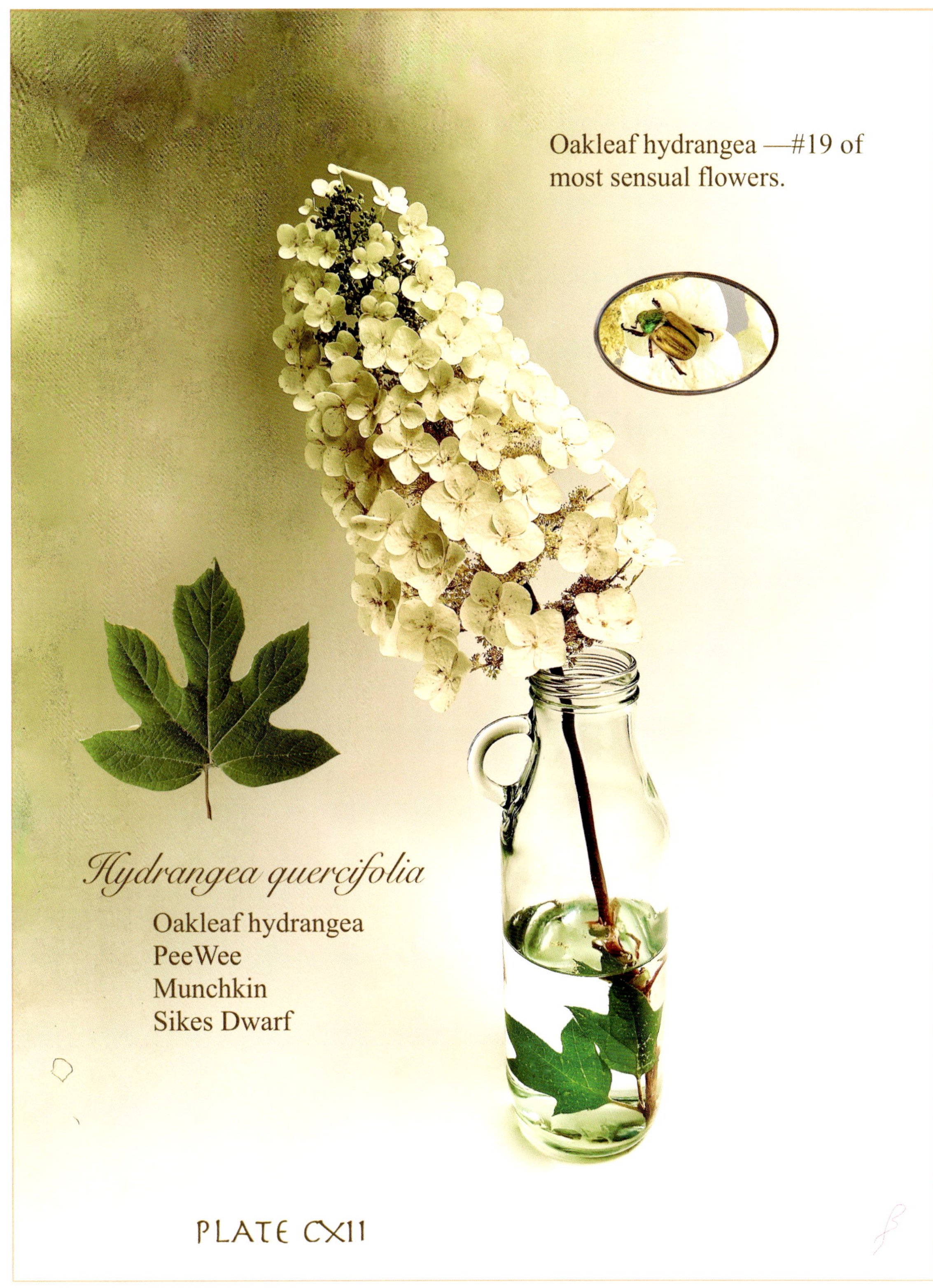

Hydrangea quercifolia

Oakleaf hydrangea
PeeWee
Munchkin
Sikes Dwarf

PLATE CXII

Do not send me roses

Roses do not surprise

Lavish me with sweet hydrangeas

Their delicate bunches a feast for the eyes.

Rhonda Johnson-Saunders

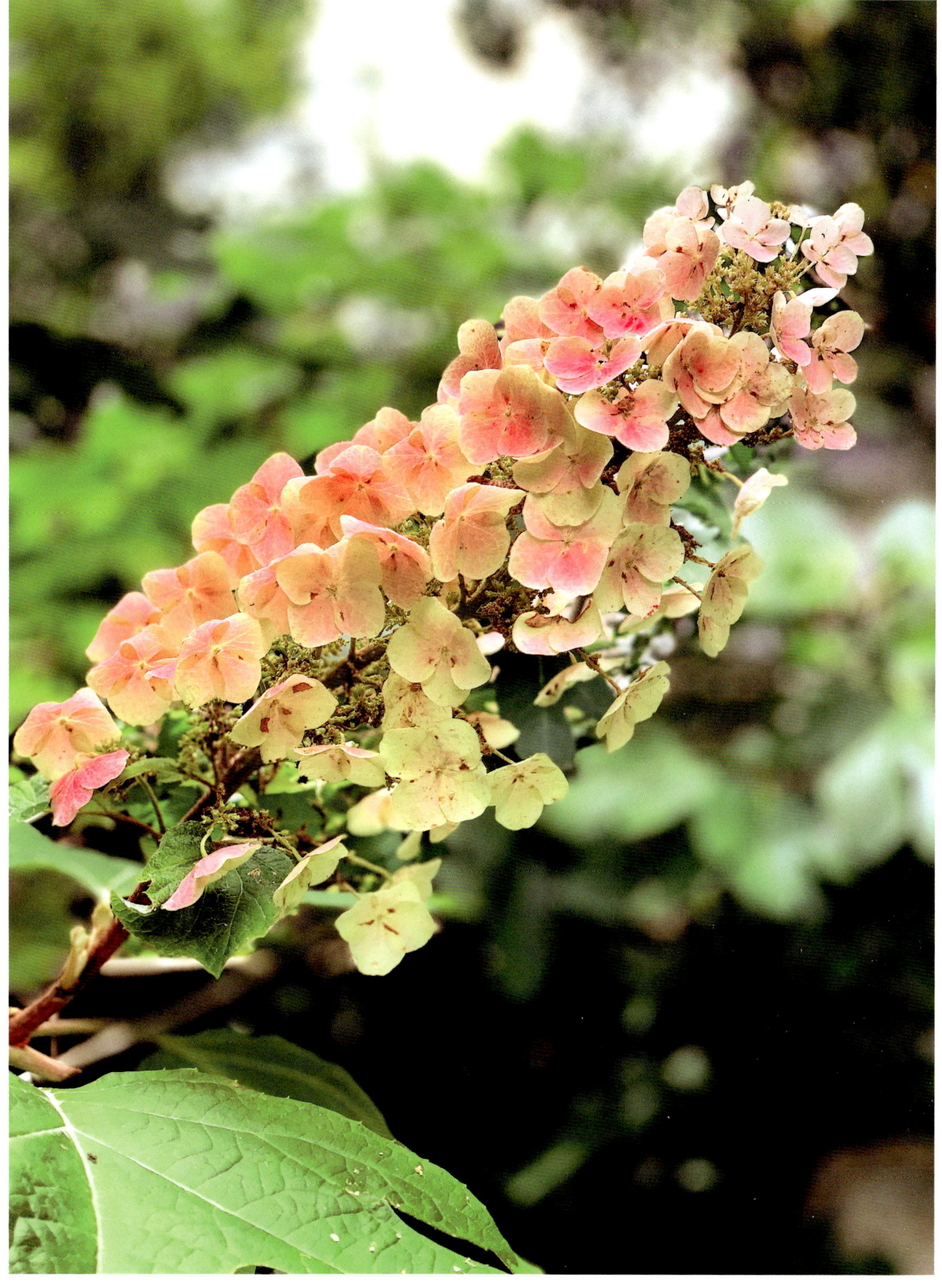

How does a pansy, for example, select the

ingredients from soil to get the right colors for the

flower? Now there's a great miracle. I think there's

a supreme power behind all of this. I see it in nature.

Clyde Tombaugh

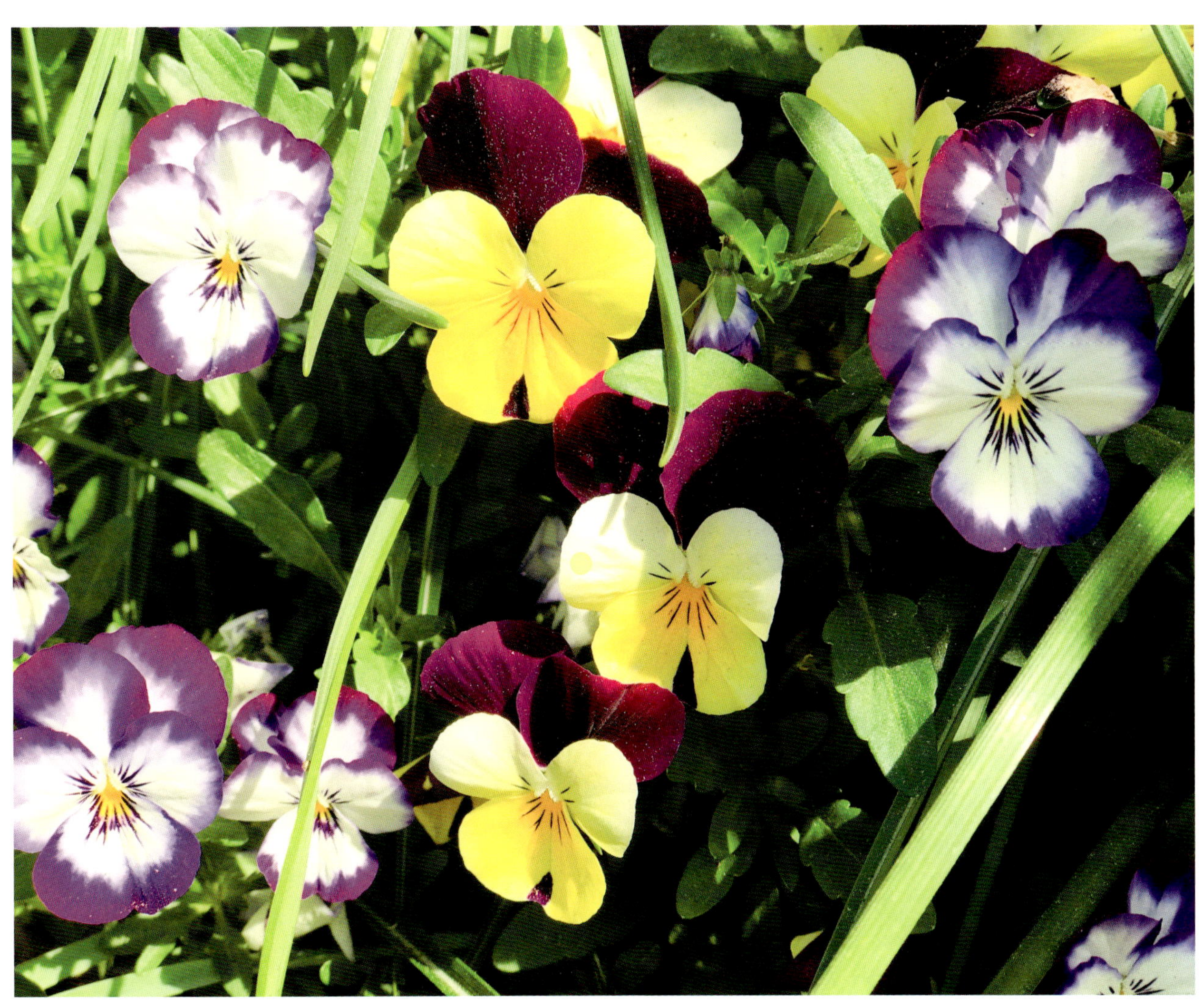

Quick sprout the Buttercups, all bright and new,

Goblets from which the fairies drink the dew.

From the Eglantine springs poetry's power –

It's the only way to describe the flower!

Rubaiyat of Omar Khayyam

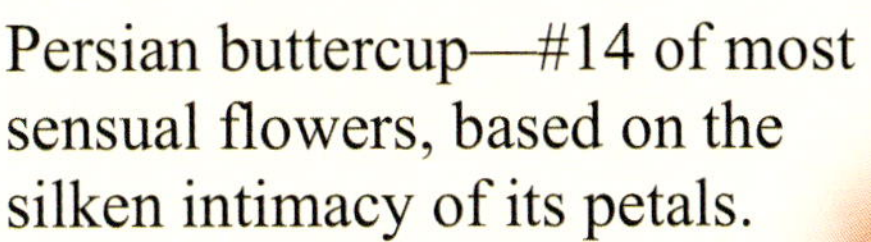

Persian buttercup—#14 of most
sensual flowers, based on the
silken intimacy of its petals.

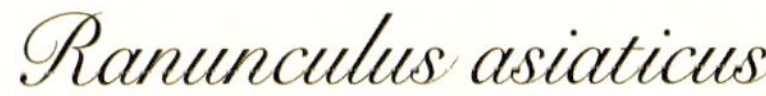

Ranunculus asiaticus

Persian buttercup
Garden ranunculus
Turban buttercup

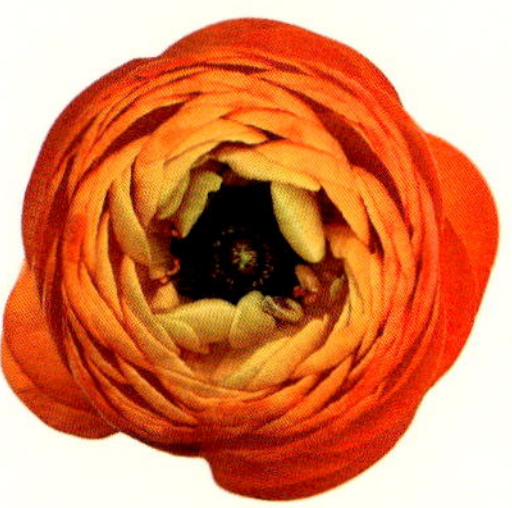

PLATE XIII

Do you remember the days

And my funny ways

As the months and years did follow?

You became my wife

And fulfilled my life

Near the place where the daffodils grow.

Do you remember the way

That we laughed all day

By the clear stream long ago.

Now you're lying here

'Neath the grazing deer

Near the place where the daffodils grow.

Charles Wiles

My heart with pleasure fills, and dances with the daffodils.

William Wordsworth

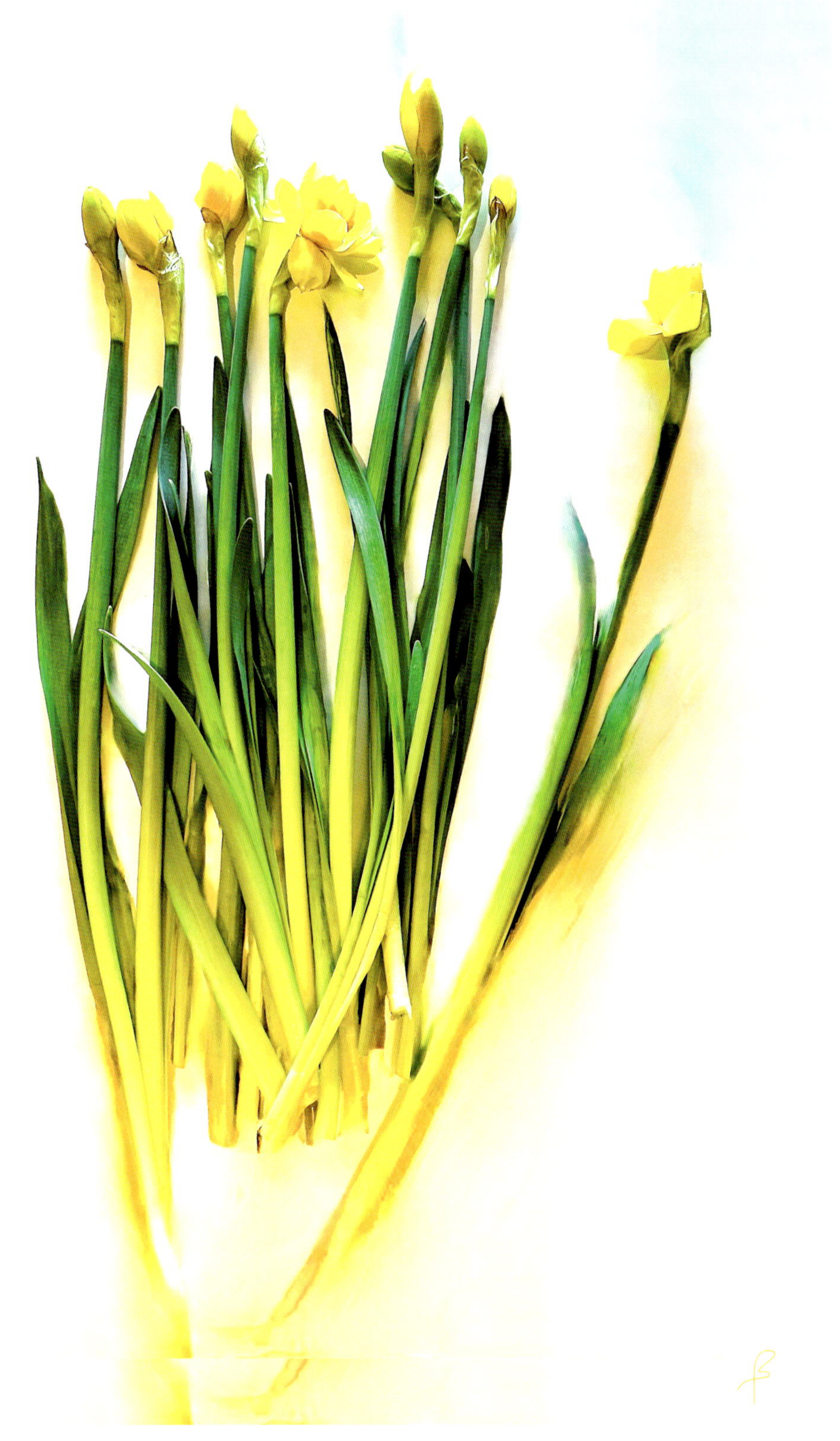

Anemone

now fly away

wasted like a

day in time

serene wanderings

to the other side

reflects unusual

madness

in language

that speaks softly

of the night's

chosen foolish

gestures

now arise

like the

shadows of

impermanence

Ananda Belford

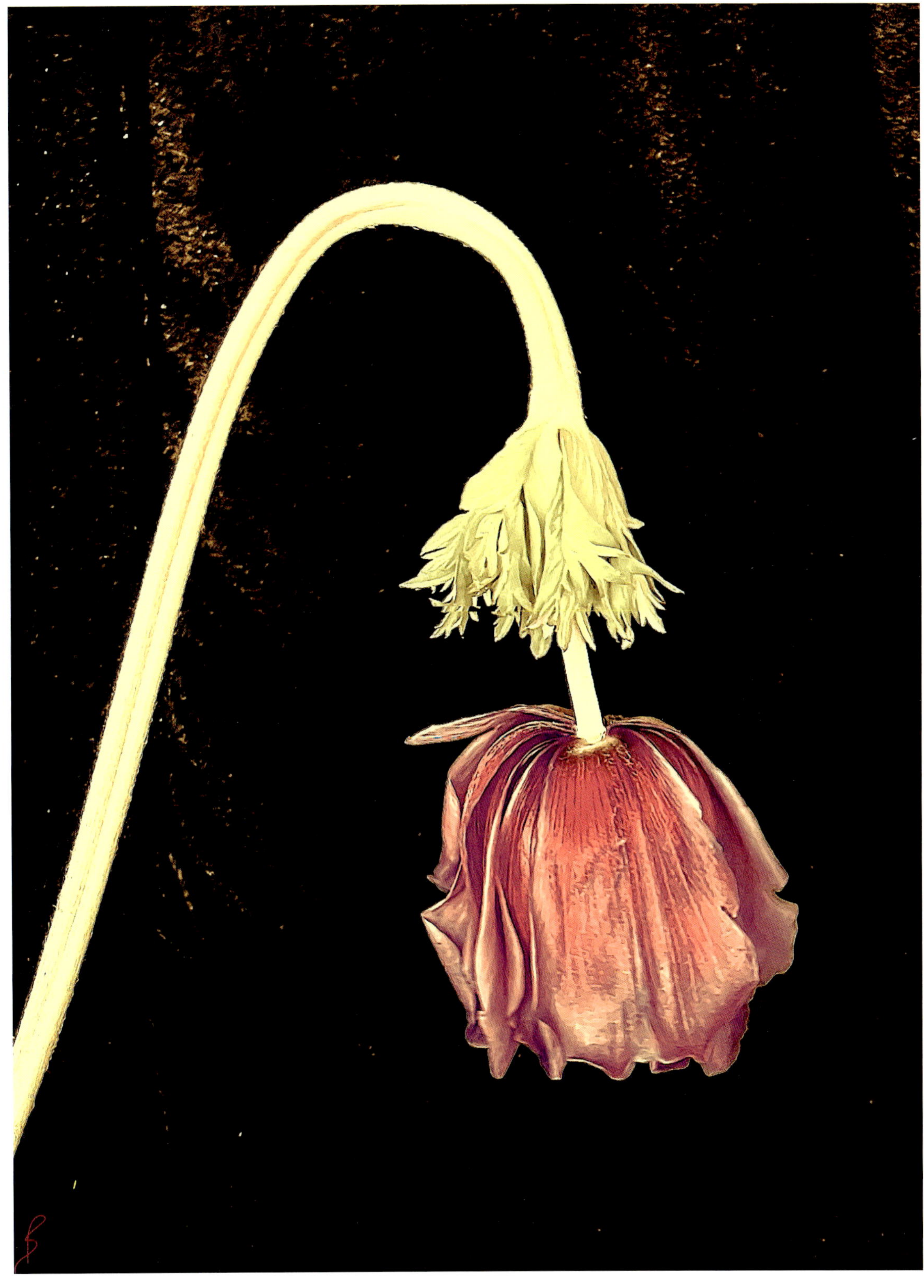

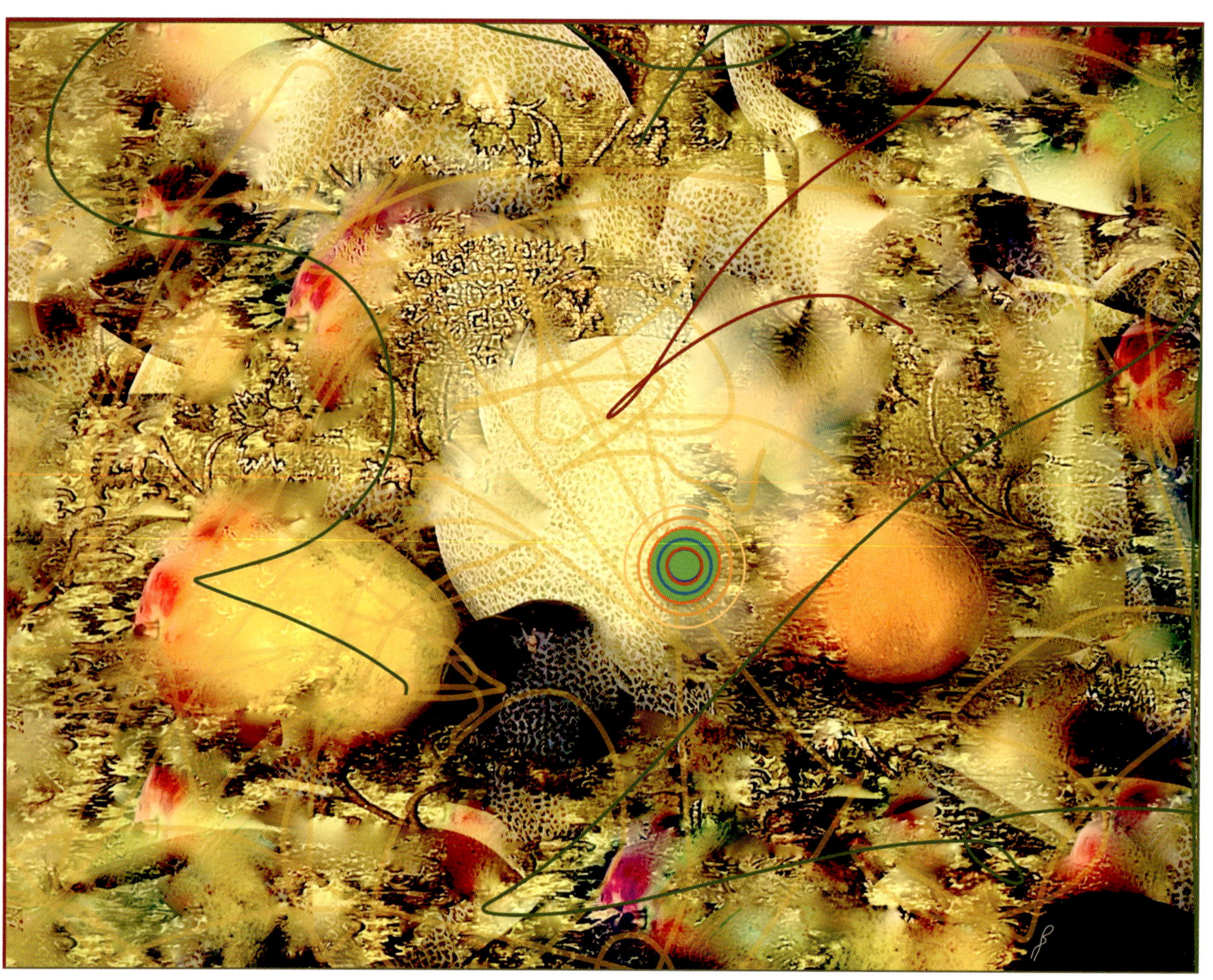

FOOD WORSHIP

There was a decade when my name was "Forever." I had long hair, did yoga and tai chai, had life–changing mystical experiences, bathed in a creek from a spring above a valley. Enveloped by forest, the creek had a slate bottom. Its water was pure.

Before moving into the valley, my new husband and I lived primarily in a Ford Econoline van we had outfitted with wood paneling, curtains, and class.

This recipe was given to me in that van. I cooked it on a two–burner Coleman camping stove on the floor behind the front seats.

This husband was with me for one more year, the recipe for five more decades.

PZS

Rice of your choice

One sizable onion, yellow or white, cut into approximately ½–inch chunks

1–2 smashed garlic cloves

Tofu, cut into ½–inch cubes

>   **Avoid the soft variety of tofu, you want the cubes to remain as cubes**

Mushrooms—handful of your favorites cut or whole

Sour cream as desired, non–dairy is good

Soy sauce—not too much, not too little

Sauté the mushrooms in butter and put aside. Sauté the onion until it becomes semi–translucent and put aside. In the same pan, sauté the tofu in oil/butter until just tan. Add the crushed garlic, cook for five minutes, then add soy sauce. Toss the mushrooms and onion on top, add sour cream and stir lightly.

Rice can be added in as an ingredient or served as a "bed" for the dish.
OPTIONAL: ½ cup of peas are a nice addition if desired.

A is for

apple

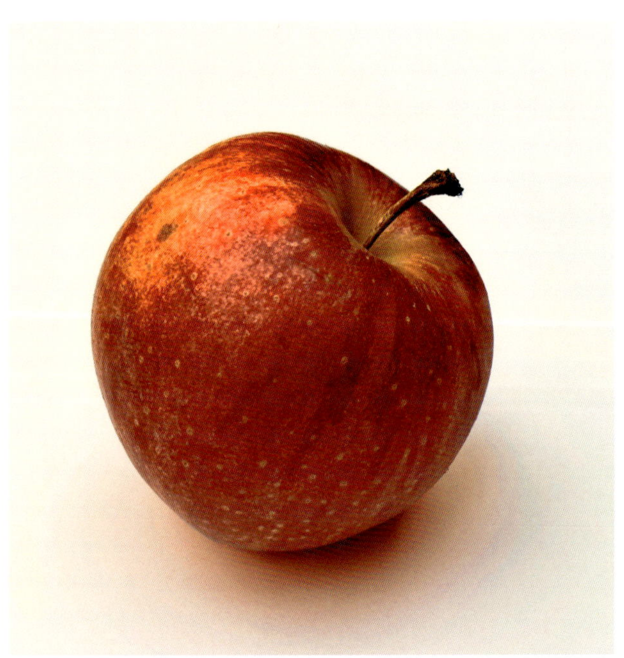

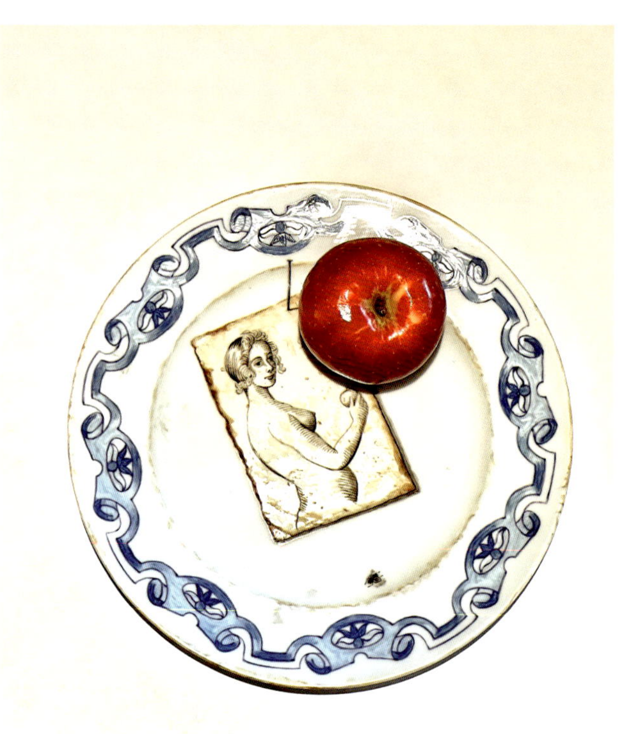

apple and adultery

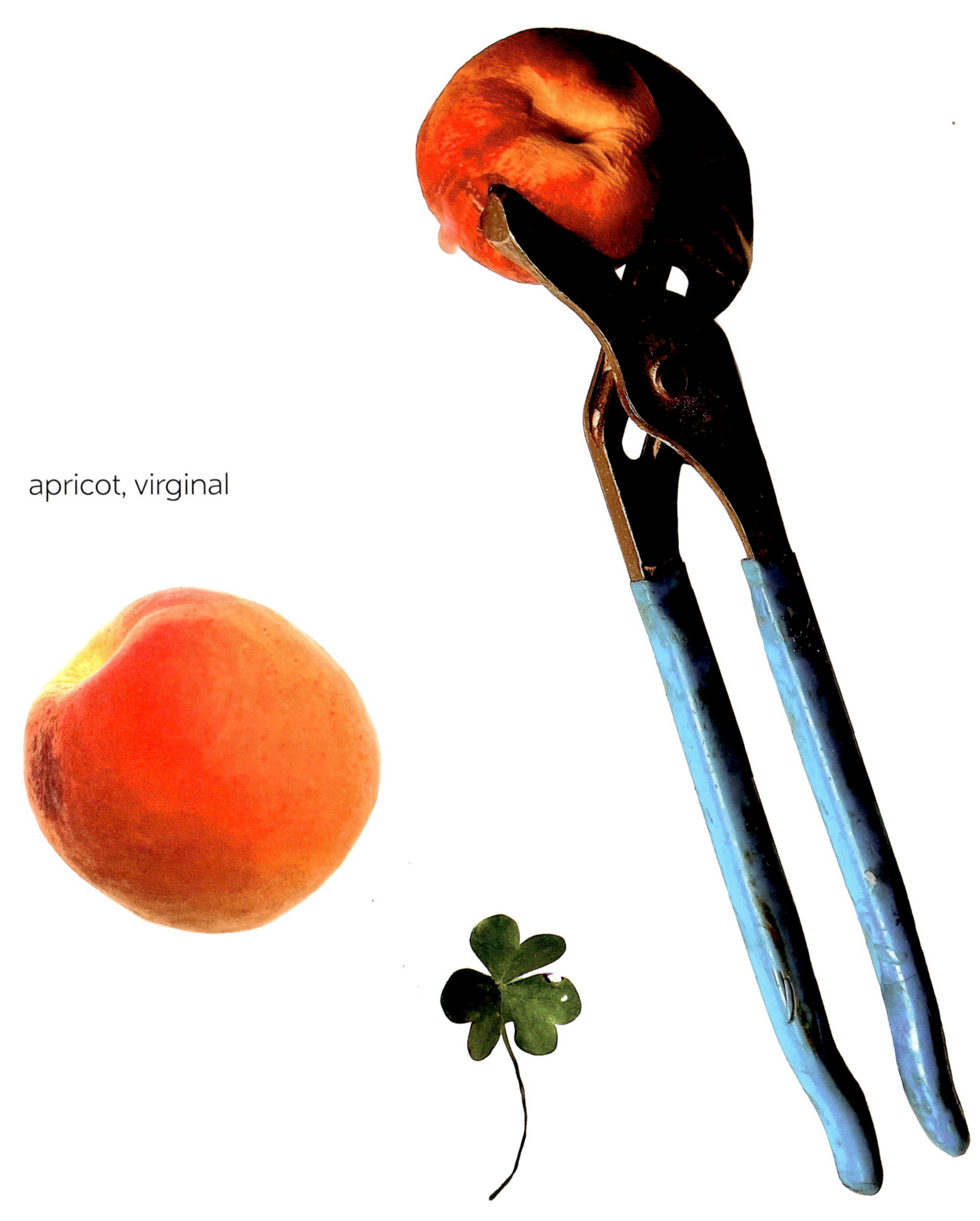

apricot, virginal

apricot, in duress

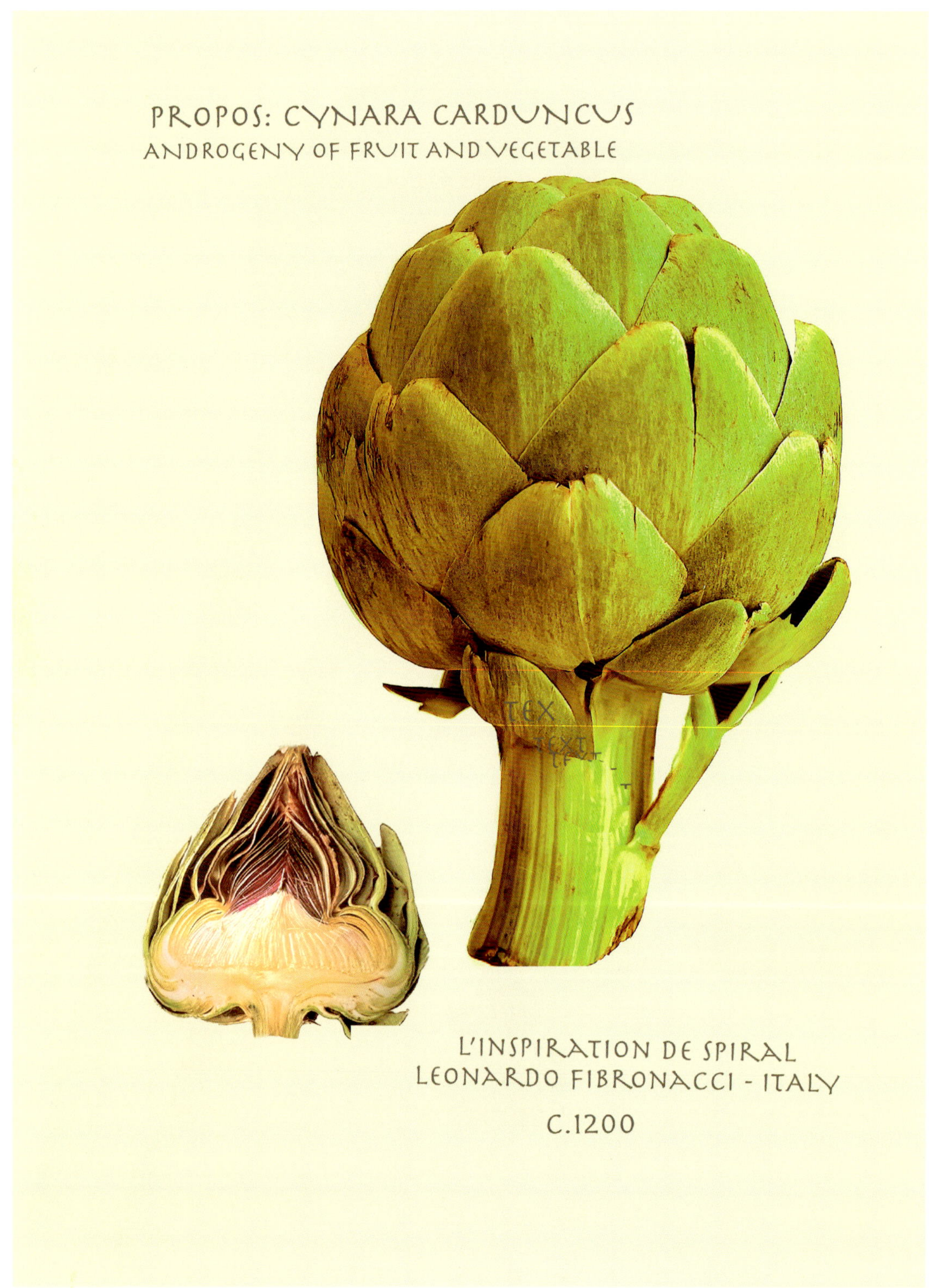

artichoke, androgynous

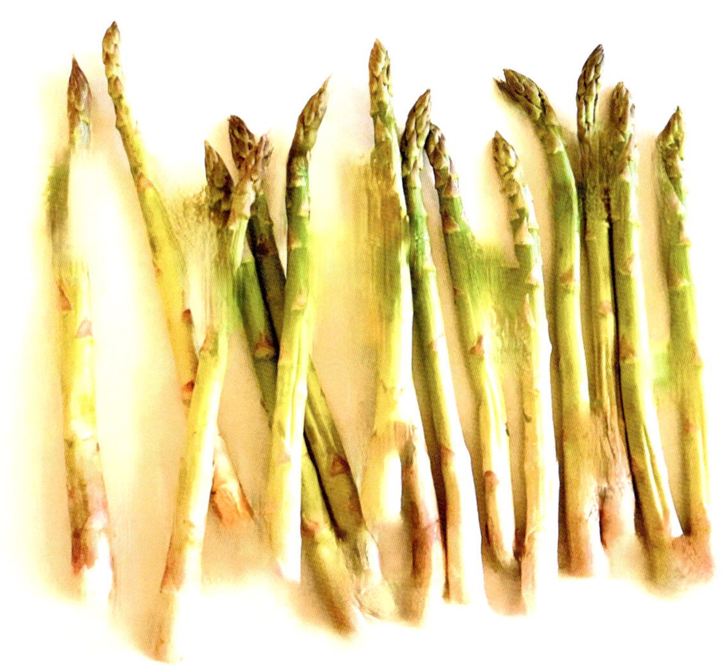

asparagus

avocado

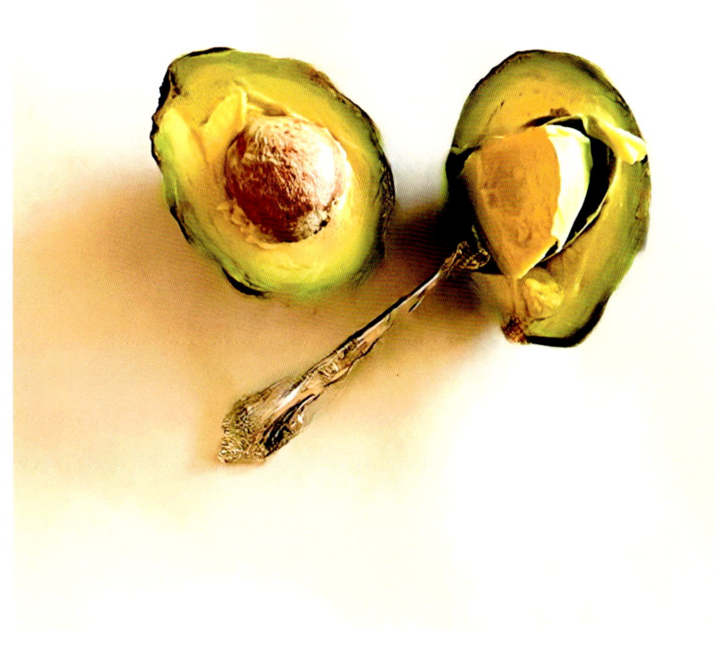

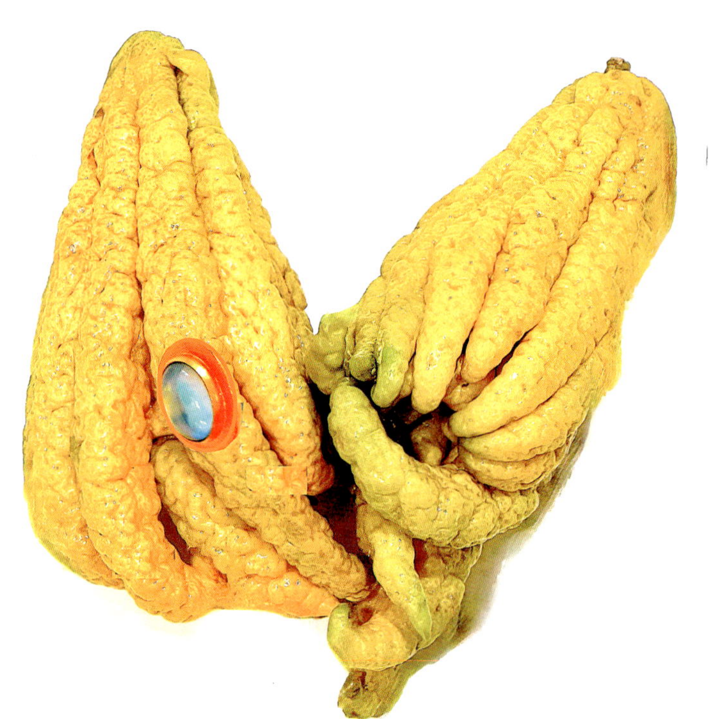

buddha's hand

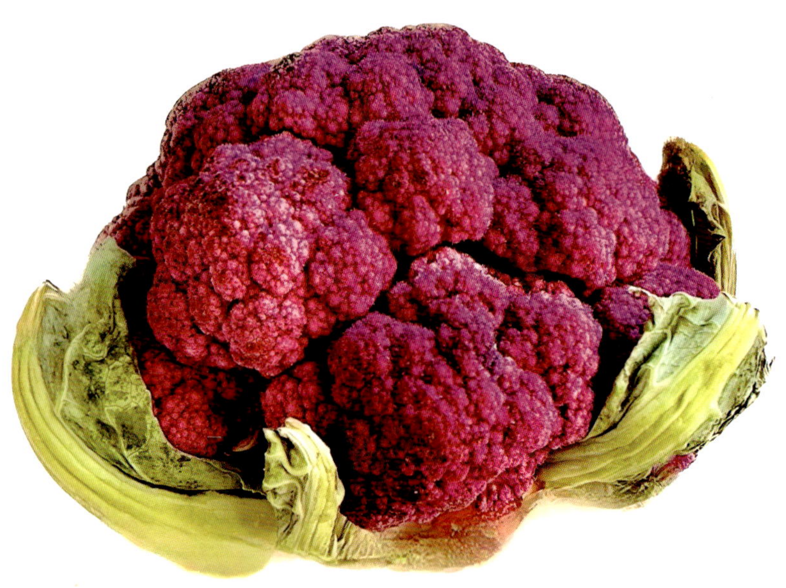

broccoli, purple

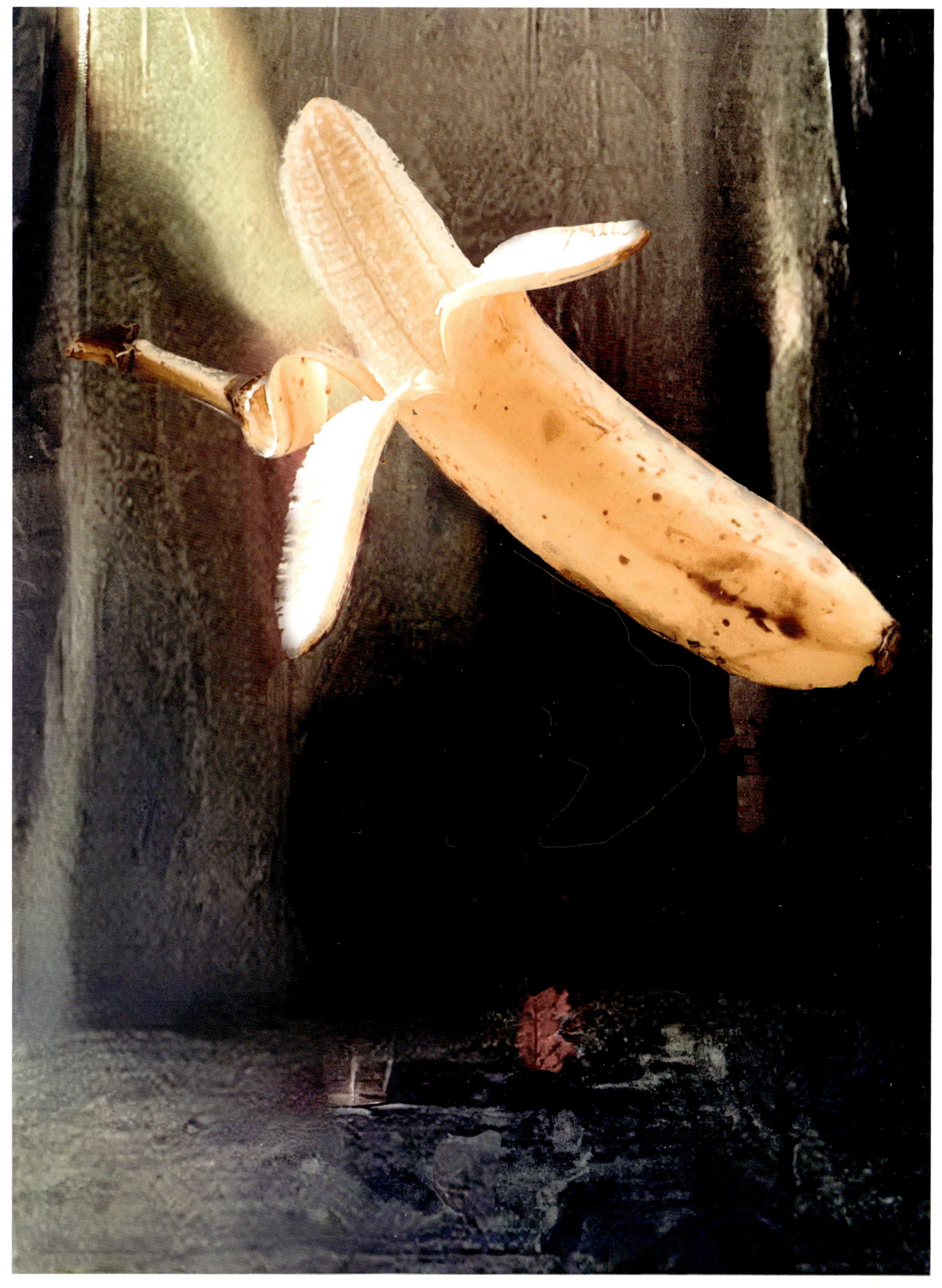

banana, ascending

Somewhere over the banana way up high

there's a land that I dream of . . .

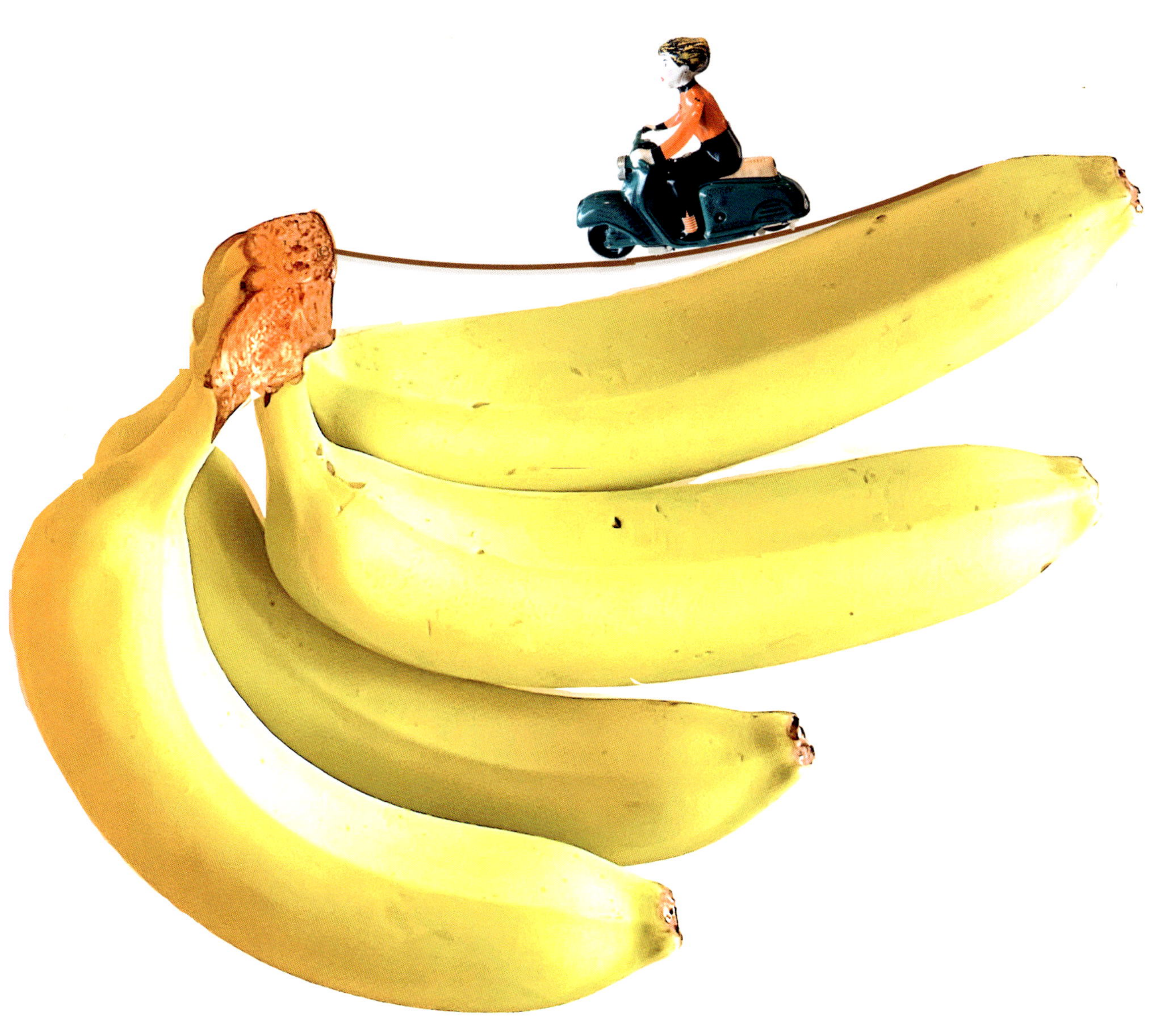

C is for

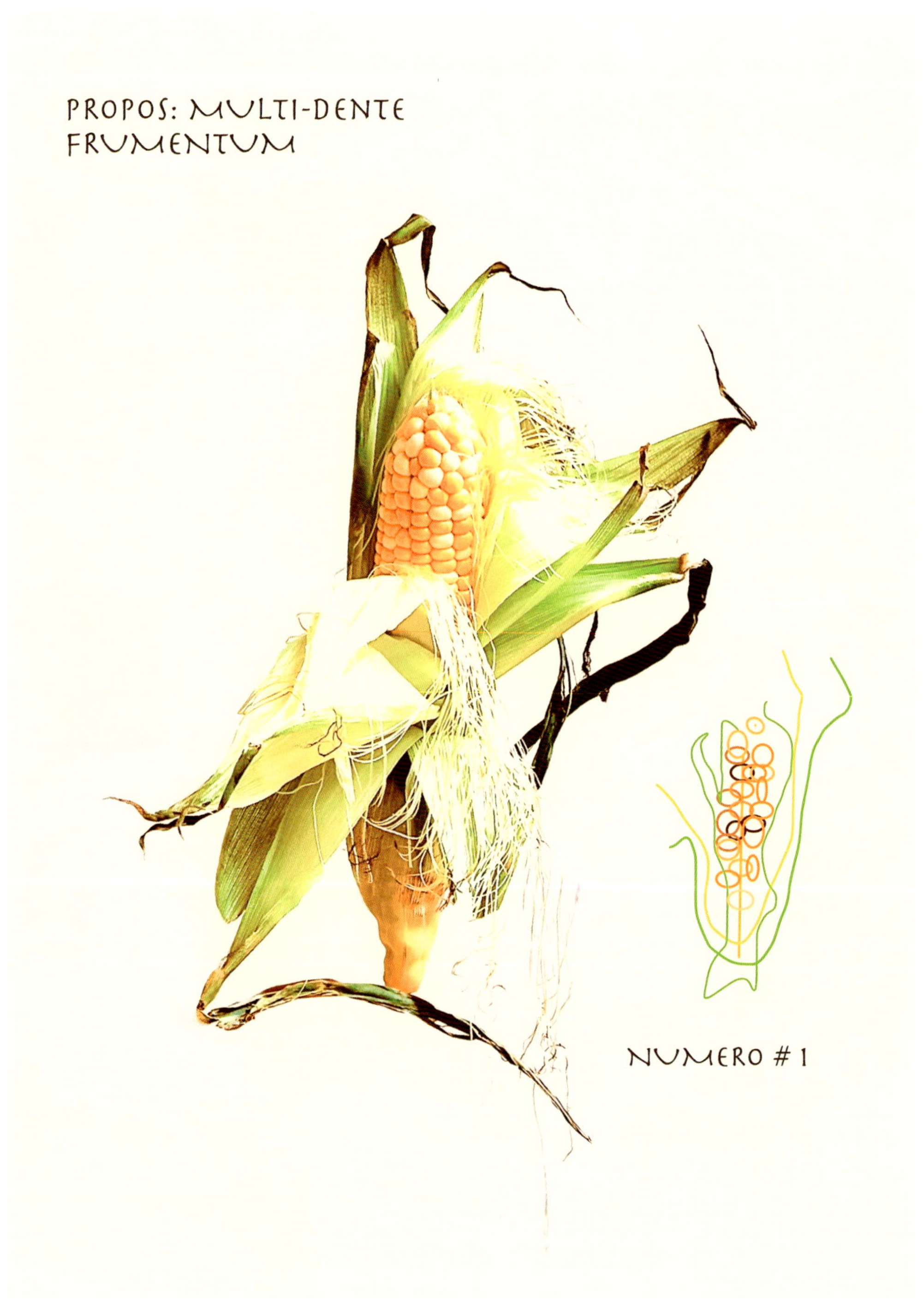

corn, farm sweet

chard/beetroot

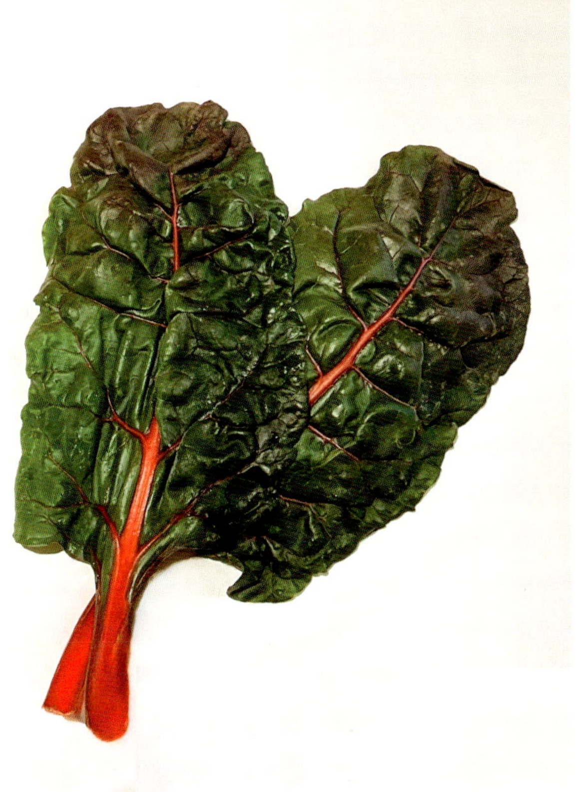

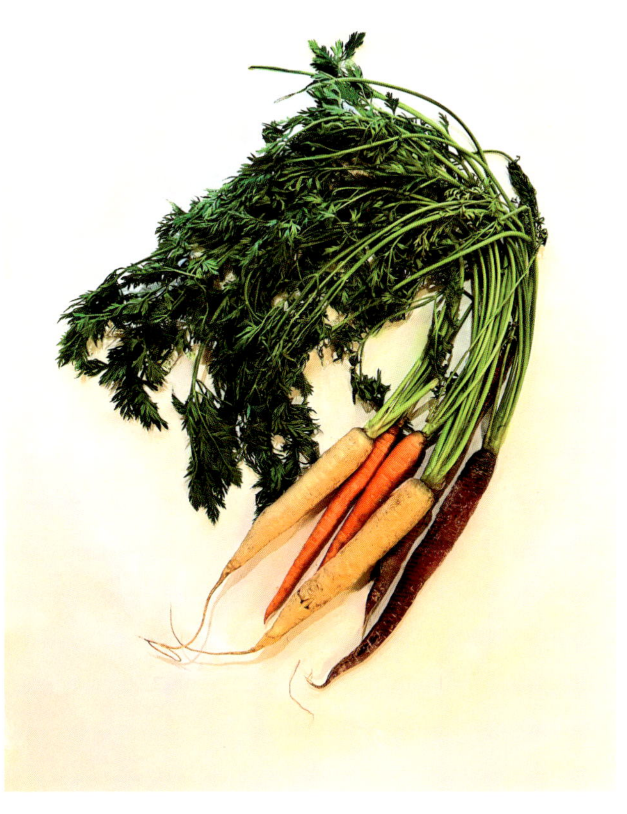

carrot, rainbow

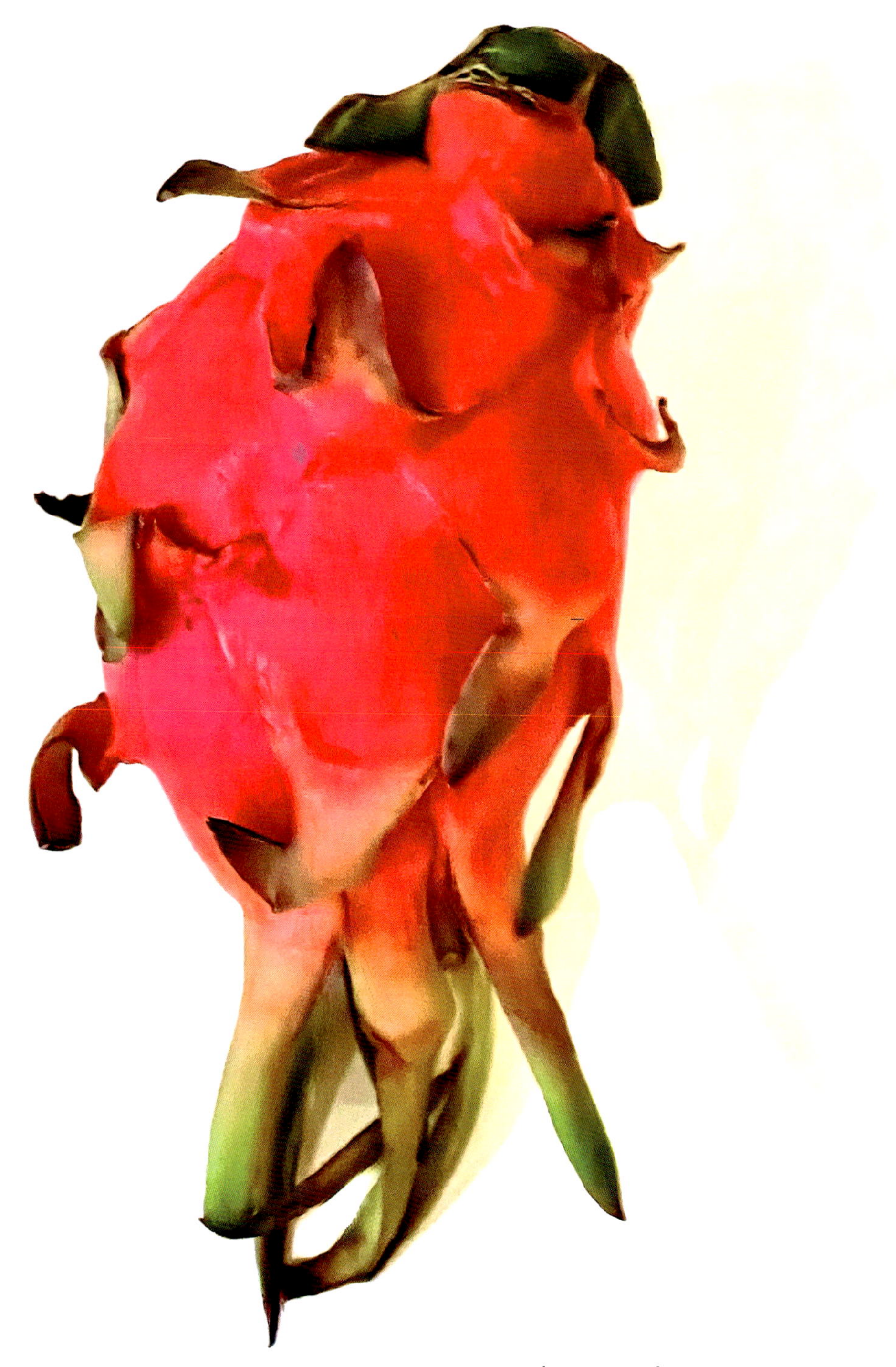

dragon fruit

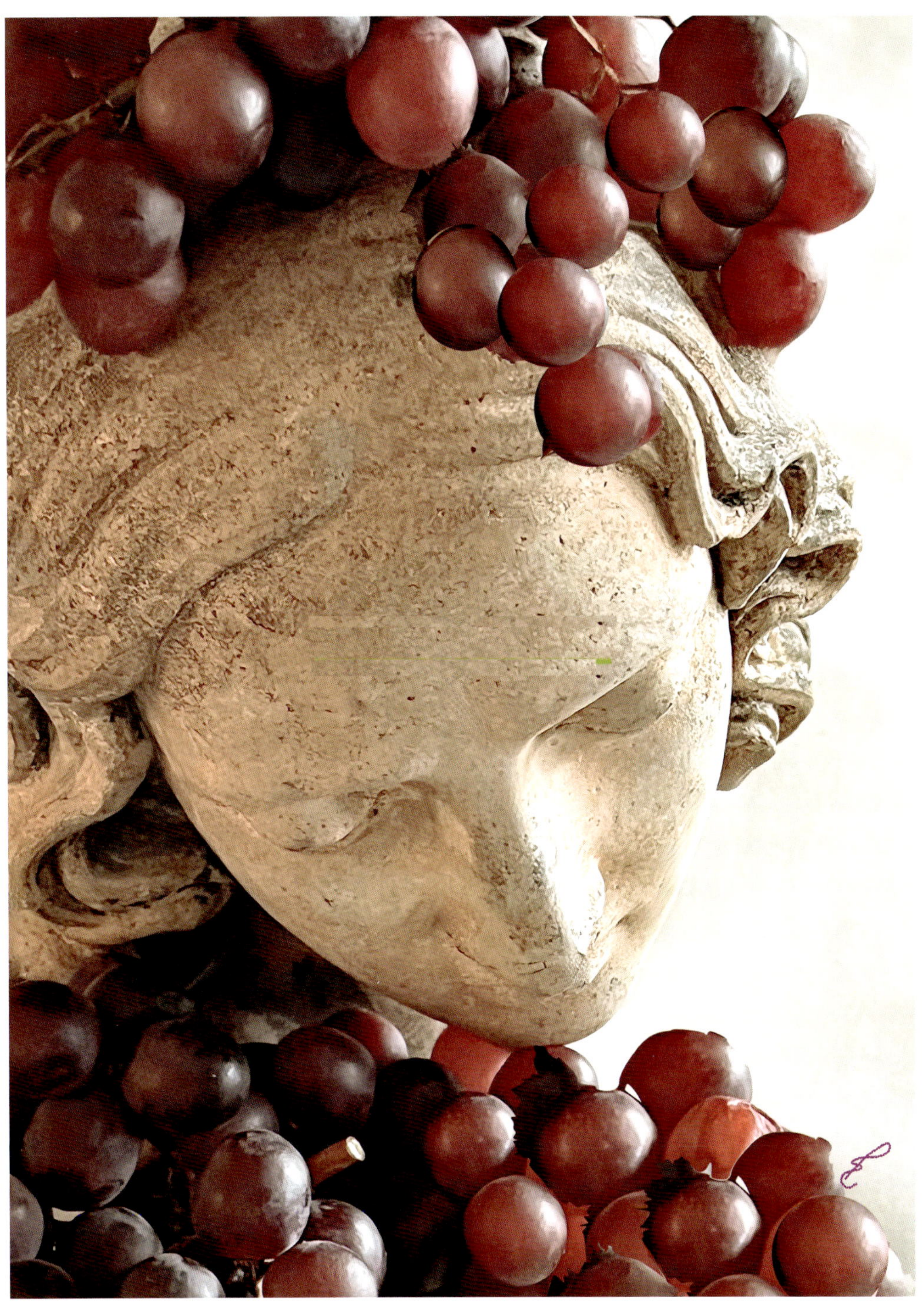

grape, common

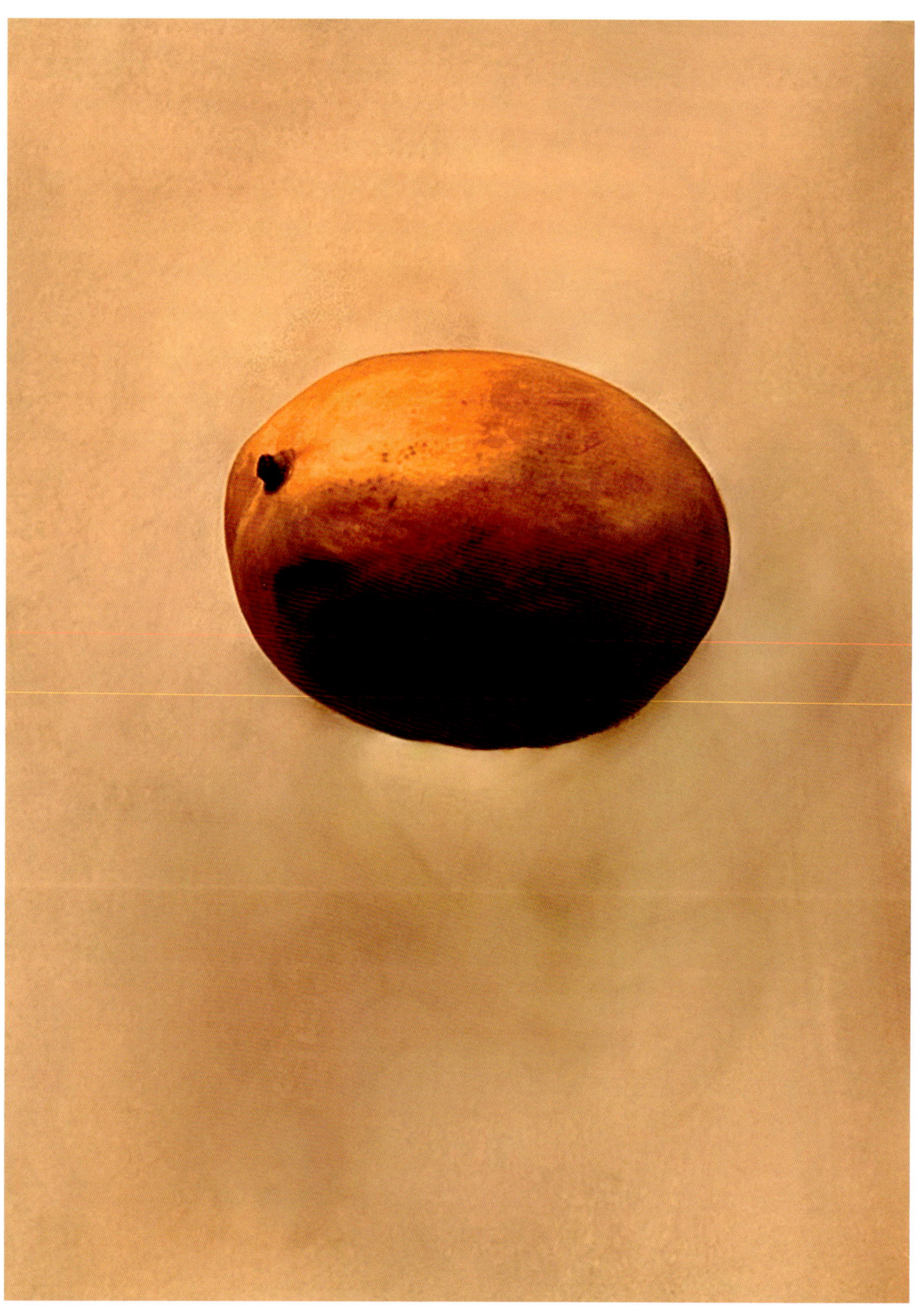

mango

O is for

onion, yellow

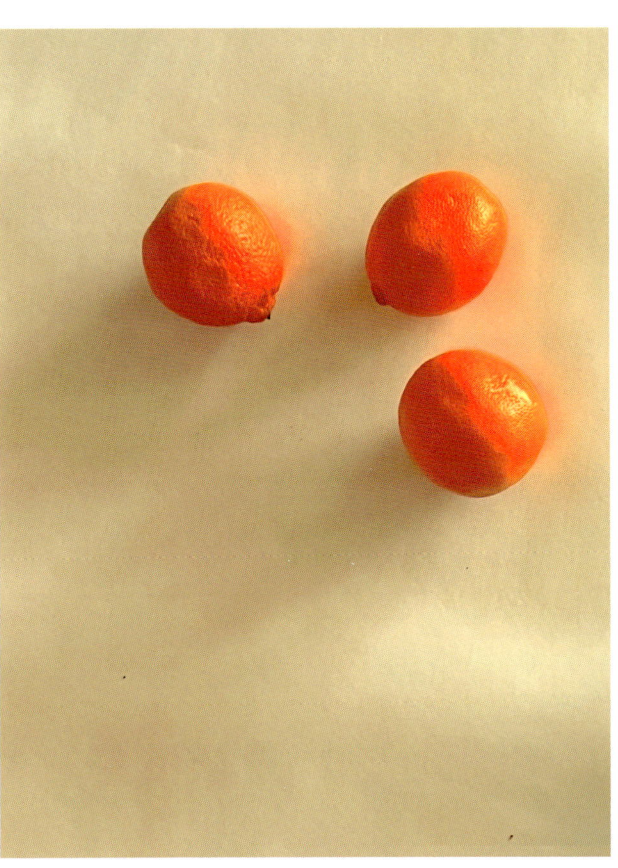

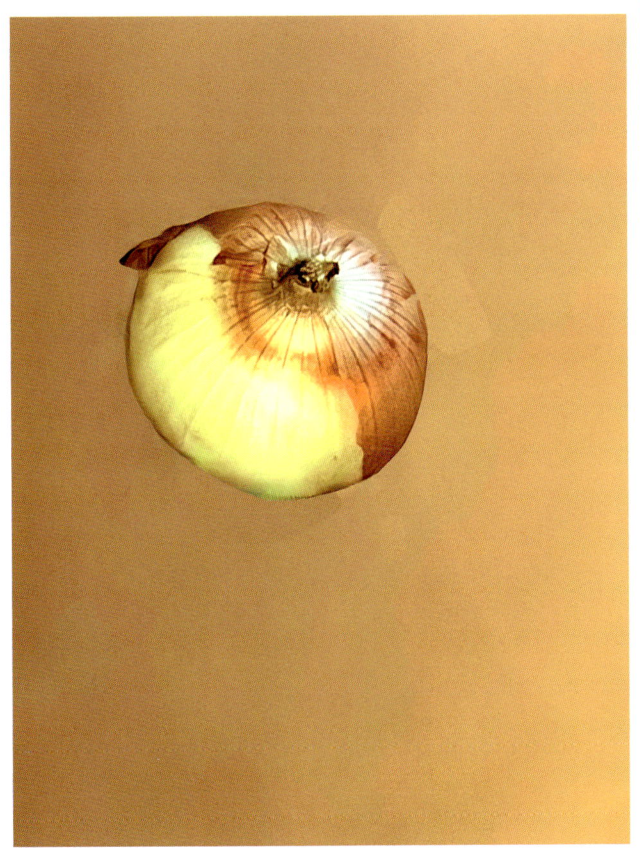

orange, orange

P is for

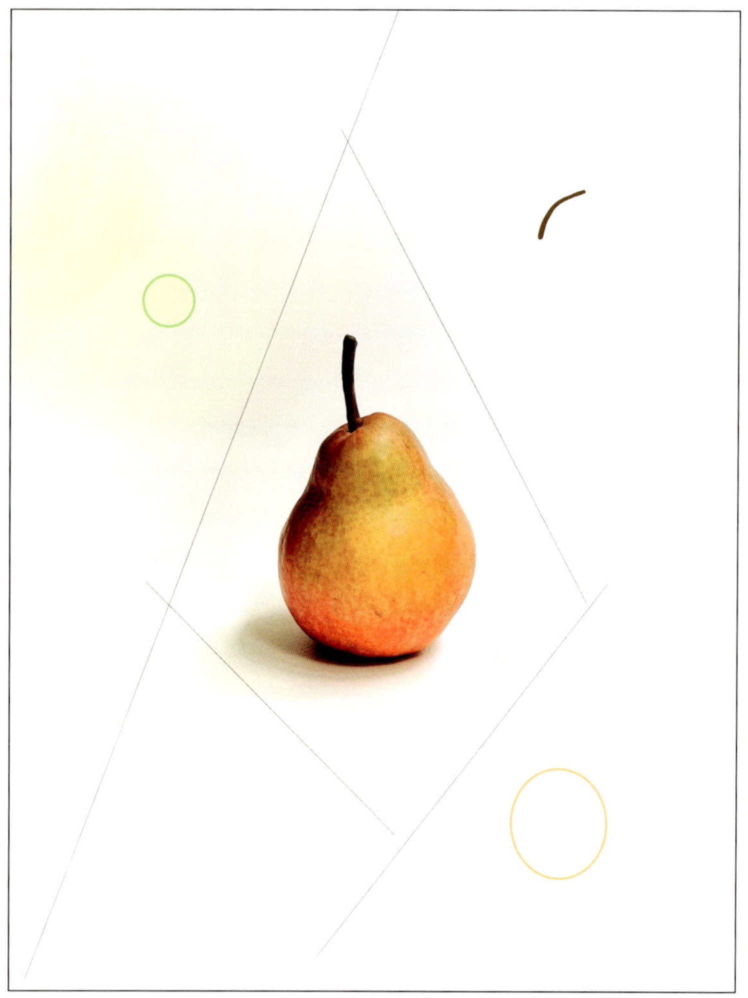

pear, bartlett

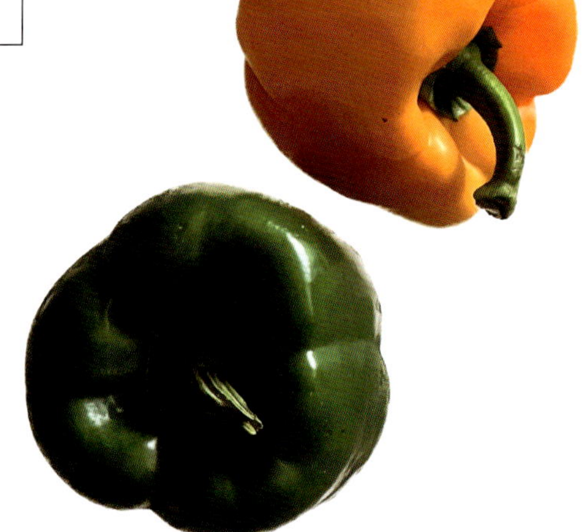

pepper, orange and green

pineapple

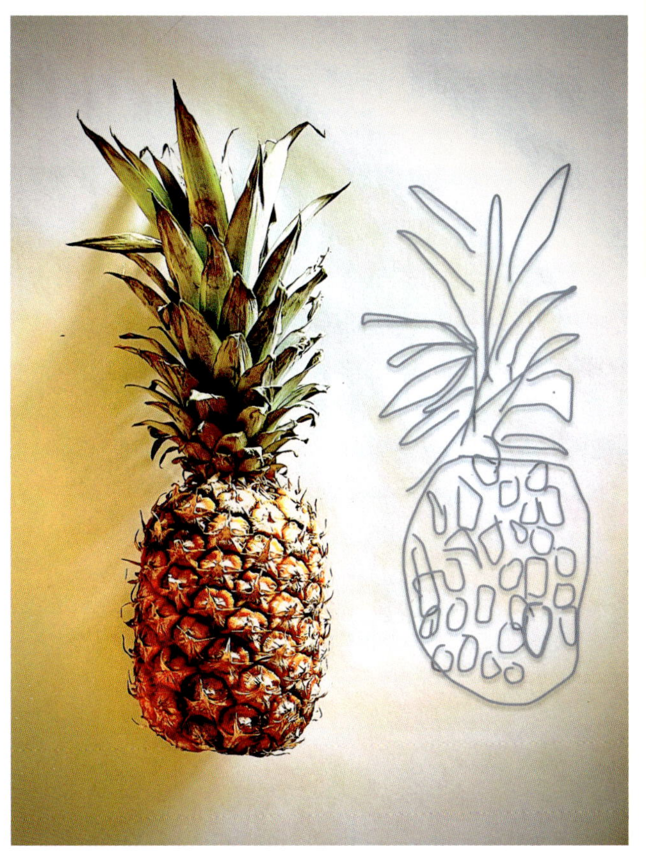

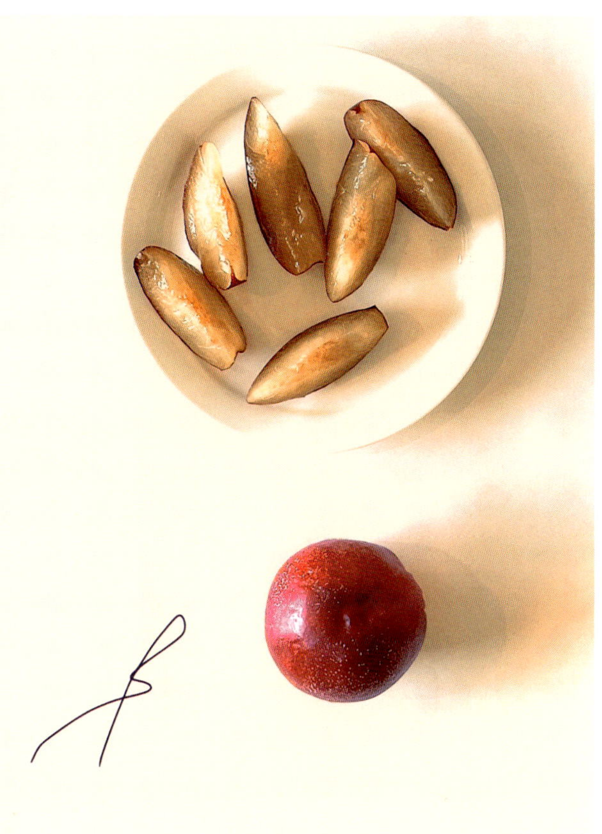

plum

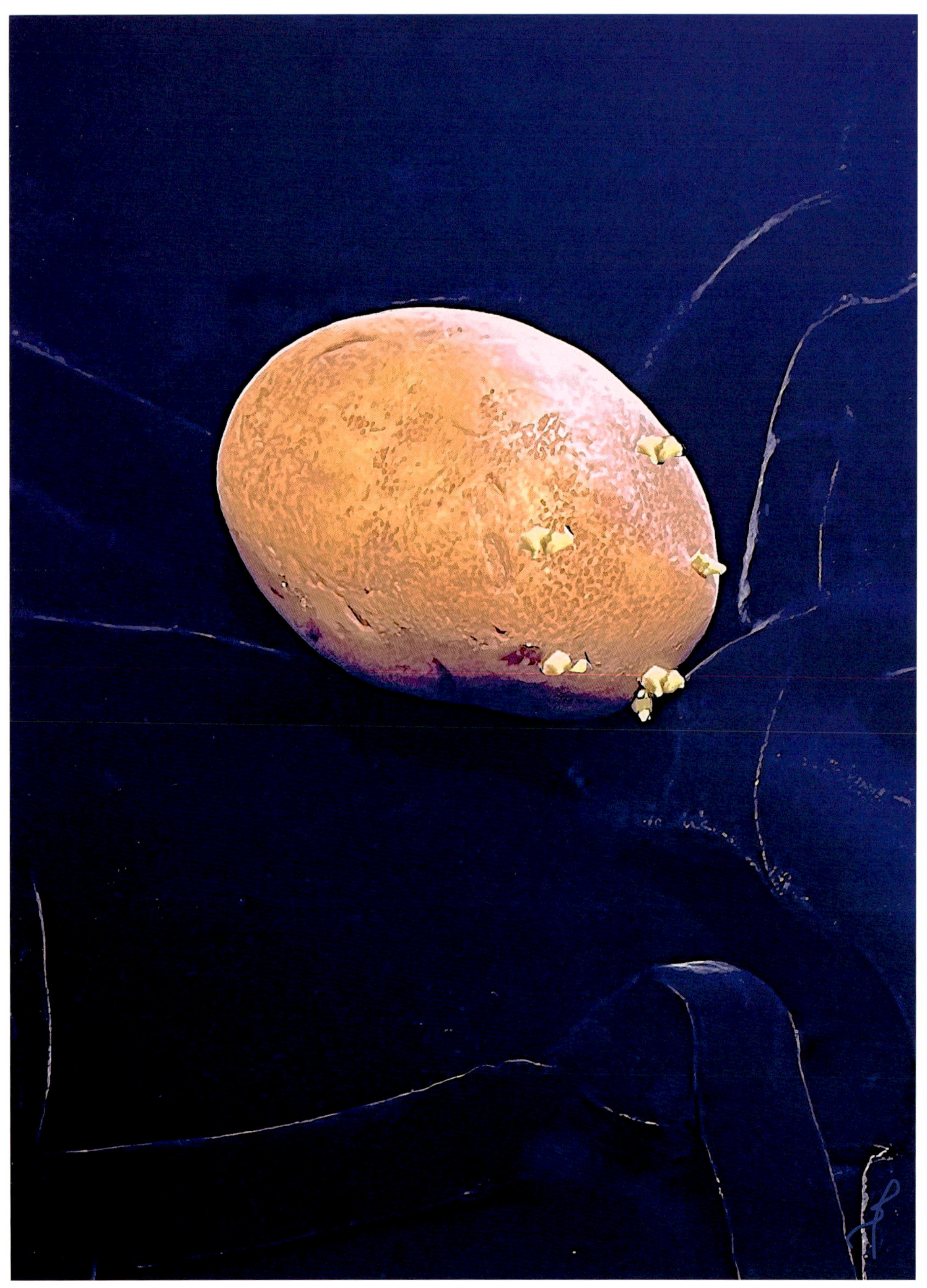

potato, on blue velvet

R is for

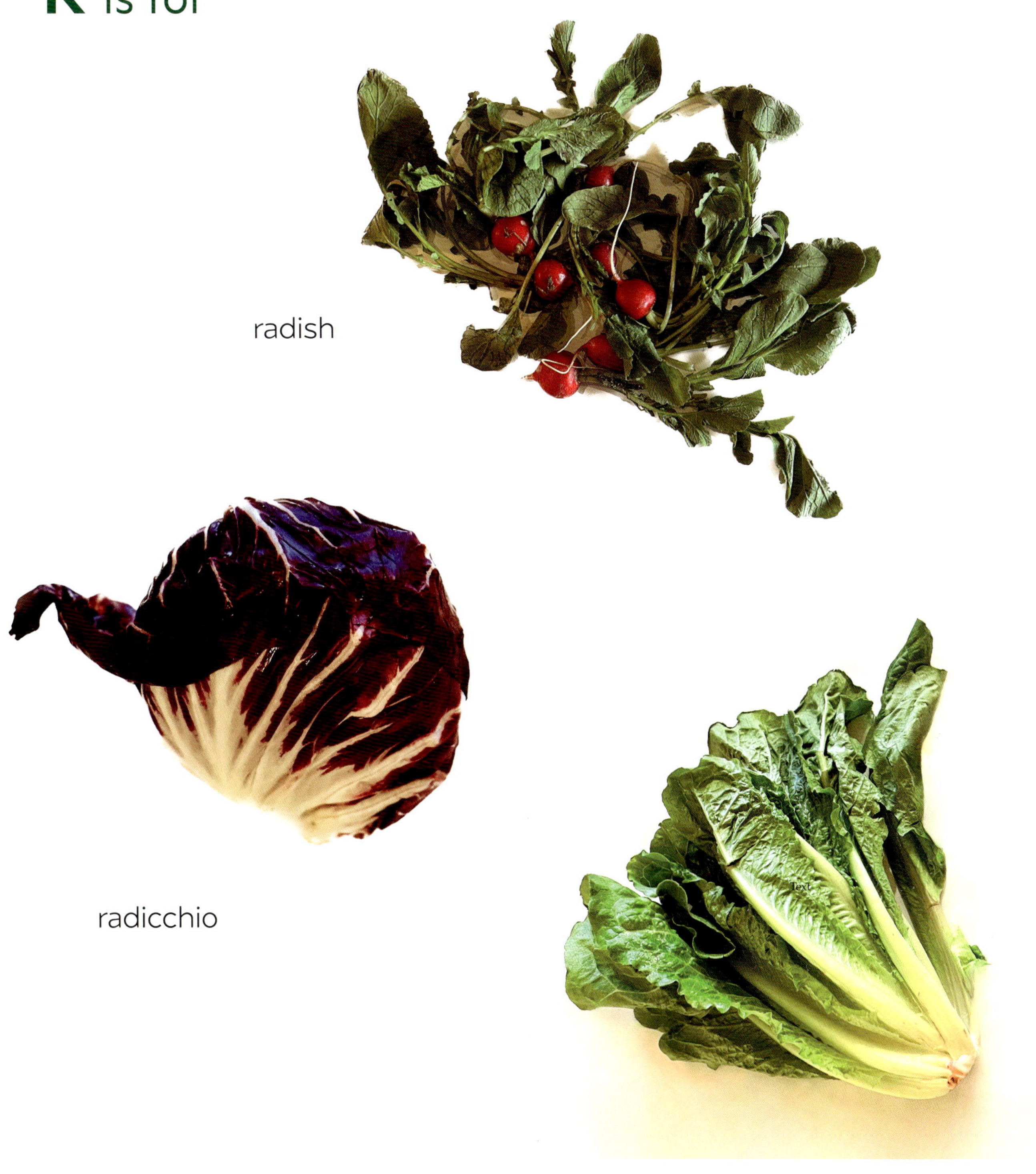

radish

radicchio

romaine

T is for

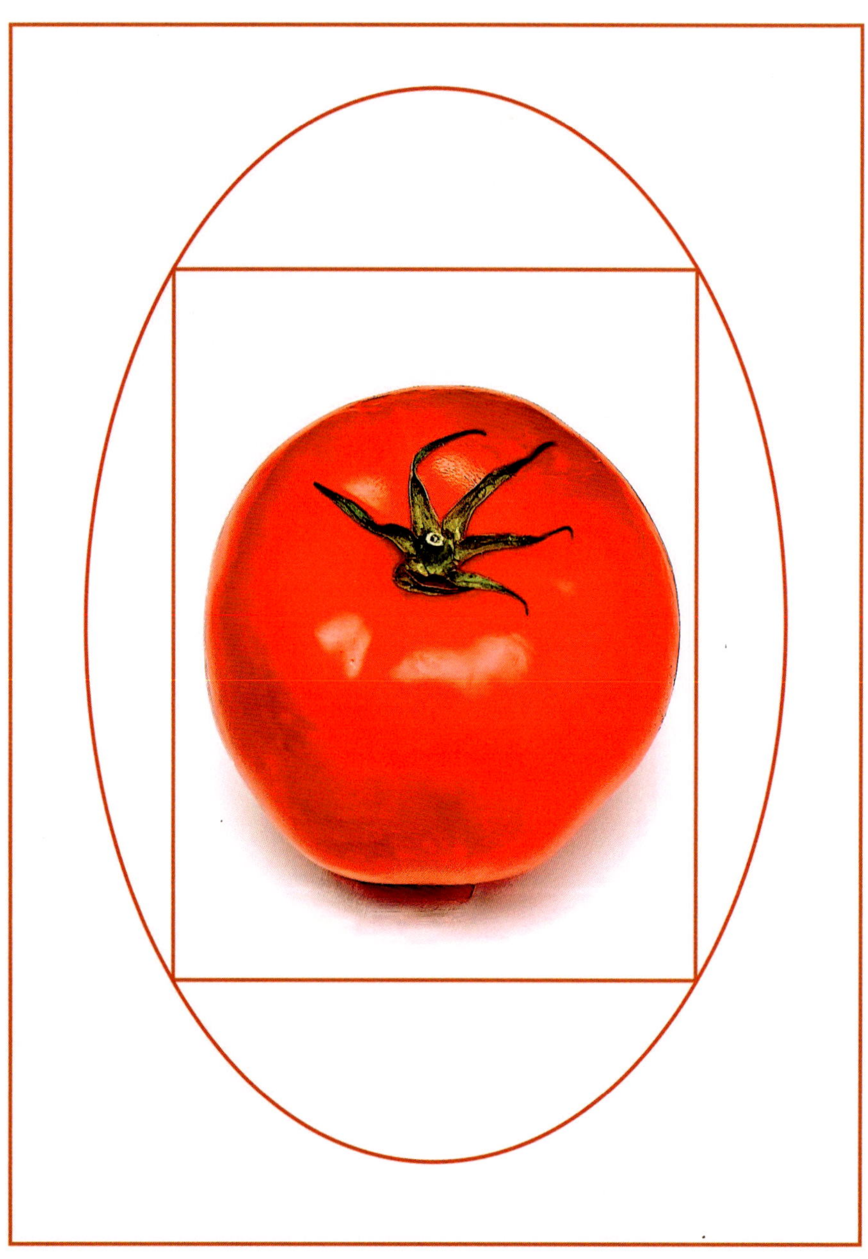

tomato

W is for

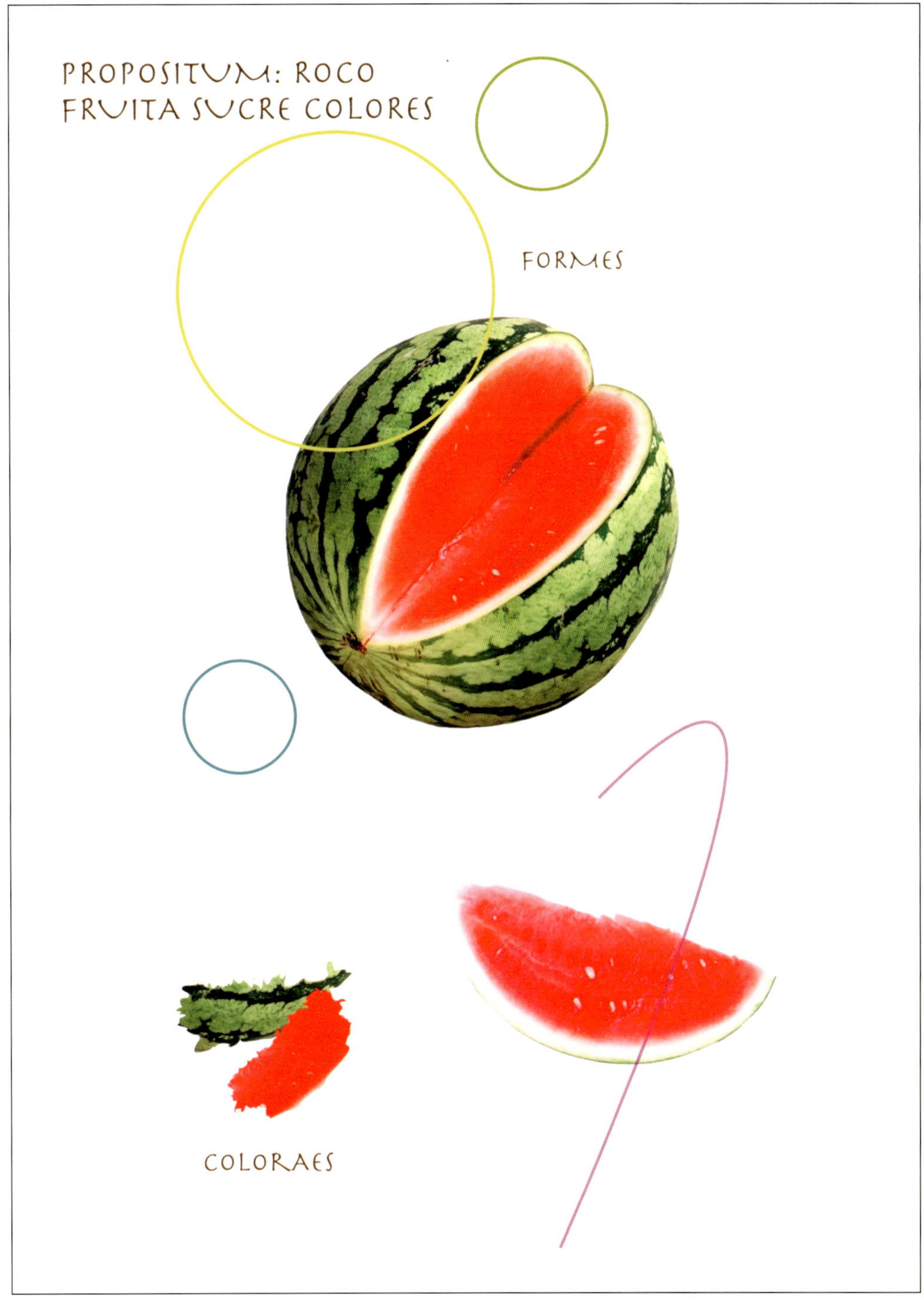

watermelon

NOTES AND GRATITUDES

A book—whether a washing machine manual, novel, history of the short life of the *Titanic*, collection of love letters, biography, guide to the mating of tropical birds—brings together thoughts and imagination in ways that we can understand—hopefully.

The added gift of this book for me was the bringing together of people supporting me as my physical and cognitive abilities declined. You came to see me, encouraged me, got me groceries, made me laugh, cooked meals, made me cry with you, got me from one place to another. You moved me into a one–level apartment from my many–staired house. You made the making of *FOREVER* a discovery of expanding connections and compassion.

I am especially grateful to my daughter Karen Celia Fox who found and scheduled caretakers, wrote an essay on time, served as editor, and helped me through the formidable tasks of this time.

I am grateful to Richard Oliver for his guidance, poems, high spirits, dozens of books, meals, and love. Richard also single–handedly found most of the poems for the flowers section.

Michael Hill renovated my new apartment and made it wheelchair accessible. Onelia Sandres and other caretakers made life much easier. Tony Dueno understands my daily need for chocolate and laughter.

I rely on Louise Brody for her meticulous care, and great eye for design. She awes me with each book we do together. I love her work and working with her.

Thank you always, Gordon Goff, for your confidence in me. The inquiry from Jake Anderson about "my next book" arrived within an hour of the dreary prognosis by my primary specialist. I had found it difficult to work for six months before then but resumed the day after hearing your message and got back to work.

PZS

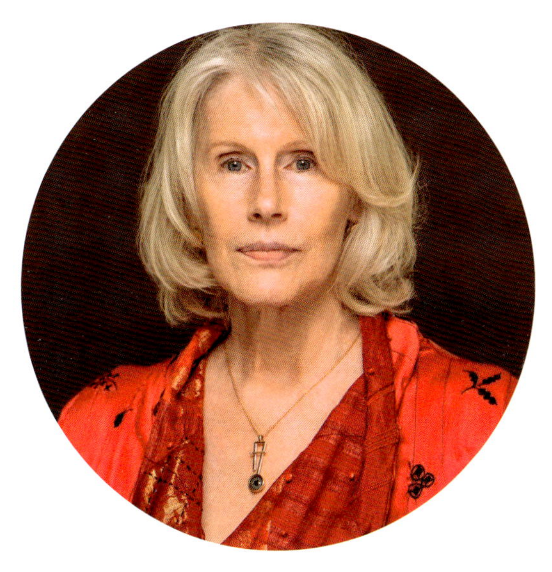

BIOGRAPHY

Patricia's life has been guided by the principle that we can learn little by common observations. Since that is true for her, she has dared to embrace risk and call up visions that do not bow to common expectations. This is evident in how she has lived and the art she creates. At this time of decreasing cognitive and motor skills, she launched her third photo–poetry book as a lifeline for herself and gift for all.

Her "photo–scapes" of all varieties bring together her sensual spiritual visions with her life experience of 81 years from growing up on a farm in Iowa and arriving to Washington, DC, at age 21 with no job, one suitcase, no place to live, and a handful of borrowed money. She became the photographer for the Office of Economic Opportunity where she led the documentation of poverty in the US. She taught photography at the Smithsonian Institution and had shows of her art photography.

She was an award–winning playwright and vintage quilt dealer with her collection of pre–1850 quilts exhibited at the Smithsonian American Art Museum. In 2002 she founded and directed the first global social network NGO matching women in the US with women in 120 other nations for secure private conversations.

She was editor, photographer, and interviewer for the book *SIXTY YEARS SIXTY VOICES: Israeli and Palestinian Women* and Executive Director of the award–winning documentary "Peace by Peace: Women on the Frontlines" filmed by an all–female crew in Afghanistan, Bosnia, Burundi, Argentina, and the US. The film debuted at the United Nations and aired on PBS.

Photo: Max Hirshfeld, 2021

Goff Books

Published by Goff Books. An Imprint of ORO Editions
Gordon Goff: Publisher

www.goffbooks.com
info@goffbooks.com

Author: Patricia Z. Smith
All photographs by Patricia Z. Smith
Foreword by Karen C. Fox
Book design by Louise Brody
Managing Editor: Jake Anderson

10 9 8 7 6 5 4 3 2 1 First Edition

ISBN: 978-1-961856-28-8

Prepress and Print work by ORO Editions Inc.
Printed in China

Goff Books makes a continuous effort to minimize the overall carbon footprint
of its publications. As part of this goal, Goff Books, in association with Global
ReLeaf, arranges to plant trees to replace those used in the manufacturing of the
paper produced for its books. Global ReLeaf is an international campaign run by
American Forests, one of the world's oldest nonprofit conservation organizations.
Global ReLeaf is American Forests' education and action program that helps
individuals, organizations, agencies, and corporations improve the local and global
environment by planting and caring for trees.